STEP ONE:

Guitar for Beginners

Book One: The Method

Cover photograph courtesy of the Randall Wallace Collection

Order No. AM 983598
International Standard Book Number: 0.8256.3451.2

Exclusive Distributors:
Music Sales Corporation
257 Park Avenue South, New York, NY 10010 USA
Music Sales Limited
8/9 Frith Street, London W1D 3JB England
Music Sales Pty. Limited
120 Rothschild Street, Rosebery, Sydney, NSW 2018, Australia

Printed in the United States of America by
Vicks Lithograph and Printing Corporation

Music Sales America

DISTRIBUTED BY

HAL•LEONARD®
CORPORATION

7777 W. BLUEMOUND RD. P.O. BOX 13819 MILWAUKEE, WI 53213

CD Track List

Contents

Introduction

I don't think I'll ever forget the feeling I had the day I bought my first guitar. I bought it from an old Greek gentleman who collected and traded guitars from his tiny apartment in New York's Greenwich Village. I picked out an ancient Washburn guitar, built around 1910. That guitar would be considered quite a collector's item nowadays, but that didn't matter to me then.

I left his little shop walking on a cloud, the guitar clutched firmly in my hand. But on the way home I stopped dead in my tracks. A cold sweat came over me. I owned the guitar. Now what would I do? I didn't have the slightest idea. I couldn't tune it, make chords, strum it, or use a pick. I had just spent my last dollar—with one subway token left in my pocket—for a guitar I knew nothing about.

I only knew one thing for sure. I loved guitars. And I loved guitar music—from folk and blues to rock and classical. Any guitar music was all right with me. I had grown up on the tight rockabilly strumming of the Everly Brothers, had gone to high school listening to Chet Atkins, had taken my first driving lesson with Eric Clapton on the radio, and had studied for finals with the classical sounds of Julian Bream on my stereo. I knew I wanted to play. I wanted to play so badly I could taste it . . . feel it. But where to start?

There's an old joke that goes: "Excuse me, can you tell me how to get to Carnegie Hall?" The answer: "Practice!" It's a corny joke, but somehow it stuck in my mind the day I bought my guitar. I went home and glanced at a bunch of chord diagrams a friend had written out for me. I carefully began to follow his instructions, stretching the fingers of my left hand across the strings on the fingerboard. It seemed to take forever, but after a while I had figured out an E chord. Triumph! A small step for mankind! Yet when I strummed across the strings with my right hand, I was in for a rude shock. The sound that came out was a cross between a rooster crowing and fingernails scratching across a blackboard. If it took this long to make one simple chord, I thought, it might take an eternity to play well. I called my friend in a state of panic. He had been playing for about six months, but he answered my questions like an expert.

"You have to be patient," he said. "Rome wasn't built in a day!"

"But how long did it take Jimi Hendrix to learn?" I asked.

"It doesn't matter," he replied coolly, "you're not Hendrix!"

Undaunted, I decided to try the guitar again. In a few hours I had learned three basic chords, shaky though they were. I was on my way. The only problem was that my fingers were very, very sore.

"What did you expect," my friend asked, "that the guitar would play itself?"

So, with sore fingers, a great deal of confusion, and some degree of frustration, I continued to chip away at the mysteries of my guitar. Am I ever glad that I did. The instrument literally changed my life. It has brought me more pleasure, more satisfaction, and more pure joy than anything else in my life—with the possible exception of chocolate.

Looking back, I recall the feeling I had when I first tried to make chords, strum, or use a flatpick. Each small victory seemed to enrich my life in ways I'd never dreamed possible. That's why I am happy to pass on some of the things I've learned to you. I hope this book will be helpful—and fun to use. I know that it all seems like a big mystery to you now—but keep on pickin', I promise the effort will be worth it.

Oh, by the way, when it comes to playing guitar, all of us are, in a way, beginners. I have been playing for twenty-five years and I still find many new techniques and musical ideas waiting to be explored. I'm sure that all professional guiarists—from George Benson to Andrés Segovia—would say the same thing: There is always something more to be discovered about the guitar!

Practicing

"A word about practicing. Don't practice twelve hours a day or anything like that. You'll just wear yourself out. Play for a while, until you get tired, and then put it down. Always make sure you are enjoying yourself. . . ."

Clarence 'Gatemouth' Brown—Blues Guitarist

Of course, you are going to have to practice. There is no getting around that. But what kind of practicing will you do? That is a very simple question, but don't underestimate its importance.

I was brought up to believe that in order to get anywhere in life, you had to work like a maniac. Perhaps that is true in business, or in the military, or in the academic world. But with music, it is another matter.

Guitar playing should be fun. It should never feel like work. If your hands don't tingle just a little before you pick up the guitar, if you don't feel a slight ticklish feeling before you practice—don't bother. Other teachers may tell you otherwise; I can't say they are wrong. But this is how I feel.

I'll never forget how much I hated practicing the piano when I was a little kid. My parents had convinced me to take lessons, but I really didn't want to. I never learned a thing, and to this day, I can barely play. On the other hand, I learned to play the guitar virtually overnight. You know why? I *wanted* to play . . . and I played *what* I wanted *when* I wanted. It just so happened that I wanted to play all of the time! I played my guitar when I should have been doing homework, when I would have been running errands, and when I should have been asleep. I hardly ever put the darn thing down.

Rick Nielson of the rock band Cheap Trick once said, "If you can't have fun with what you're doing, you really shouldn't do it." Of course, there will have to be a certain amount of *effort* if you are going to get anywhere with your guitar. But the bottom line is enjoyment. Go at your own pace, relax, and enjoy yourself.

Holding the Guitar

You've just gotten you new guitar home and you've opened the case. The guitar is staring at you, asking to be played. You reach down, grab the strings, and start to pull the guitar toward you.

"Not that way, you klutz!" the guitar screams, strings clanging discordantly. "Pick me up where the neck meets the body . . . gently."

You try again, pulling it out of the case.

"That's better," the guitar sighs. "Now put me on your lap."

"This is rather sudden," you say, stunned. "I've only just met you!"

Although later you will probably want to play guitar standing up, for now you will find it much easier to learn and practice if you sit on a nice, hard, straightback chair and hold the guitar as in the picture below. When you can play as well as Elvis (Presley or Costello) you may hang your guitar around your neck with a strap and even tapdance while you play.

Once you are seated comfortably, you will be looking down at the guitar from above. From this bird's-eye view, you will see the basic parts of your guitar. Off to your left, at the end, you will find the *peghead* with the *tuning pegs* attached. Attached to the tuning pegs are *strings* which run all the way along the *neck* to the *bridge* of your guitar. You will have to reach over and adjust the tuning pegs to tune your guitar. An out-of-tune guitar is basically worthless, and many a guitarist has been tempted to trade in or smash a guitar that won't tune properly.

The string closest to you is called the low E-string. It is the thickest string. Guitarists generally start tuning with this string—although you may want to start with another string once you are familiar with the tuning process.

"Okay, Mr. Segovia," the guitar taunts. "Let's see if you are clever enough to get me in tune."

Tuning

Bluegrass guitarists like to joke that "you can tune a guitar, but you can't tuna fish." That's certainly true. When it comes to guitar, there are several ways to tune, all of which have their advantages. As you can see, there are six strings on your instrument. They are named as follows:

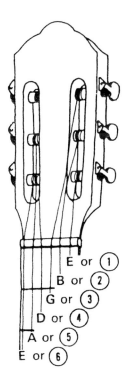

One way to tune is to play a note on the piano and then try to match the sound by turning the tuning peg until the string is properly taut. Here are the notes on the piano that correspond to each string of your guitar.

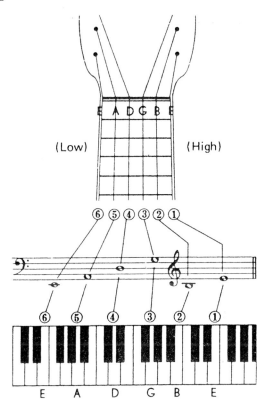

This method is good because after a while you will train your ear to hear the subtle differences between notes in tune and those that are out of tune.

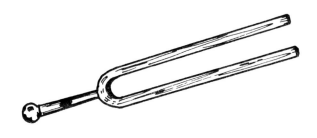

You may use a *tuning fork* to get a true A note—which, of course, corresponds to the fifth string of your guitar. Once your A string is in tune, you may use it as a reference to get the other strings in tune. The standard tuning setup of the strings on your guitar makes this an easy matter; just follow this procedure: Fret (press down) the sixth string at the 5th fret and you will get an A note. That should correspond to the sound of the open fifth string—which is already in tune. If it does not, the sixth string must be adjusted. Likewise, the fifth string at the 5th fret should equal the fourth (D) string; the fourth string at the 5th fret should equal the third (G) string, and the second string at the 5th fret should equal the first (E) string.

The third string, however, must be fretted at the 4th fret in order to equal the second (B) string. Many guitarists use this method to check their tuning when they suspect a string has gone flat (too low) or sharp (too high).

The *electronic tuning device* is one of the great inventions of modern times. It can make tuning very easy and help your ear to develop at the same time. I would recommend investing in a tuner for three good reasons: First, when you are out of tune, the tuner will tell you precisely which string (or strings) is out. Second; the tuner makes it extremely easy to get in tune with other musicians by giving a standard reference point. Third; it makes it possible to tune in noisy surroundings because you don't have to actually hear the notes—the machine indicates pitch visually. This is why you will see rock guitarists using tuners on stage where the background noise makes it impossible to tune by ear.

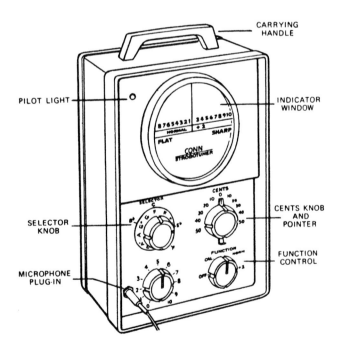

Never underestimate the importance of being in tune. As hit songwriter/guitarist Livingston Taylor once told me: "A guitarist must be perfectly in tune. There is literally no excuse in this day and age to be out of tune. A guitar in tune is a happy guitar!"

Strings

Your guitar may come with *steel* or *nylon* strings, depending on the style of guitar you have bought. Nylon strings are generally used in classical music, although jazz players like Charlie Byrd and Earl Klugh employ nylon strings for their fingerstyle techniques. Some folk guitarists use nylon strings as well. Nylon strings are good for beginners because they are easier on the fingers than steel strings.

Steel strings are generally used in country music, rock and roll, and folk music because of their twangy resonance and versatility. Light gauge strings are recommended for beginners, particularly when using steel strings. There are also very light *silk and steel* strings available that combine nylon and steel effectively. I have used these strings for quite some time and find that they sound bright and clear, and are easy on the fingers.

When choosing your strings, keep in mind that the differences between brands are slight. In fact, more expensive strings are not necessarily the best. I suggest you experiment with different types and gauges before settling on any specific type of string.

Your strings will have to be kept in good shape as you continue to play. Most professional guitarists change their strings quite often.

"My hands sweat like crazy," country-folk guitar whiz David Bromberg once told me, "so I change my strings after every show. They go *dead* (lose their bright sound) very quickly, so I have no choice."

David Bromberg's case may be a little bit extreme, but strings do wear out, or get rusty. I suggest wiping them off with a clean cloth after practicing.

Sore Fingers

Your fingers will get sore. I can guarantee that. The more you practice and play, the more they will hurt—up to a point. It is simple biology. Your soft fingertips, pressing against the thin wires of the guitar, will become somewhat sore. But don't worry. The discomfort is only temporary. It *will* go away. After a while, you will develop callouses on your fingers and it won't hurt to play.

In the meantime, there is little you can do to get around soreness. Clarence 'Gatemouth' Brown, the Grammy Award–winning guitarist from New Orleans, suggests soaking your fingers in vinegar before you play. He also recommends rubbing the juice of the aloe vera plant on your fingertips after playing. "That will take away the soreness," he claims.

Chords

Let's put aside further technical talk about guitars until later and get down to some playing. We'll start by looking at a diagram of the fingerboard.

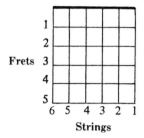

As you can see, this diagram represents a straight-on view of the fingerboard. Each string has a number, as you can see under the chart. The frets are also numbered, beginning with the fret closest to the nut (represented by the thick line on top).

Of course you will be using your left hand to play notes and chords, so we will need numbers for your fingers as well.

A note is a single string played by itself. It may be the third string, or the fifth—and it may be fretted by pressing down with a finger of your left hand, somewhere along the neck. Let's try to fret the fourth string (called the D string) at the 2nd fret, using the first finger of the left hand. On the diagram it looks like this:

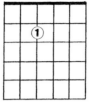

Now, let's hold that note and add two others below it, both at the 2nd fret.

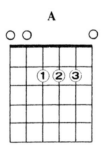

This is an A chord. Now, with your right hand, brush down across the strings near the sound hole. Can you hear all of the notes? Are they ringing clearly? Or is it a muffled mess? If it sounds jumbled, you must adjust your fingers so they press down correctly.

Let me give you a few pointers on how to hold your left hand so that the chord rings out properly. Place your thumb on the back of the guitar neck, to give your hand strength and leverage.

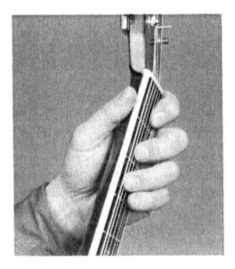

Now, make sure your fingers are pressing the strings very close to the fret, without actually being on the fret. You shouldn't have to push too hard, but give it enough power so that the notes are clear. If your sound is muted you probably need to exert more pressure. By the way, the nails on your left hand should be cut relatively short to prevent them from interfering with clear tones.

Your right hand, for now, should simply curl up slightly and strum down lightly across the strings. We'll get into more complicated strumming soon, but for now just brush down.

As an alternative stroke, you might want to slide across the string with the fleshy part of your thumb, hitting one string at a time. Your right thumb will play a very important part in your playing later— particularly if you play fingerstyle folk music or jazz.

So, let's try the A chord one more time, before moving on to our second chord, the E chord. The E

chord is one of the richest first-position chords you will learn, and you will probably find yourself reaching for an E chord time and time again. It looks like this:

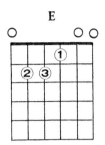

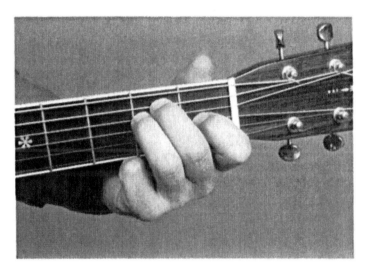

Try strumming across the E chord. The clue to playing guitar lies in your ability to change chords at will. Try going back and forth from the A chord to the E chord. Here is how this simple chord progression looks in rhythmic notation:

Each slash (✔) represents one beat in a four-beat measure of music. So every time you see the slash, give it one downward strum. Do this until you can change chords easily and cleanly without losing the beat.

There is one more thing I must mention. When you play an A chord, try to stay away from the low E-string. At times it will sound fine with an A chord, but it may also sound dissonant or harsh to the ear. You will certainly hear this as you play.

John Henry

Now you are ready for your first song. I thought I'd start with a bluesy folk song called "John Henry" because it has always been one of my favorites. I've always had a deep love for the blues, and while this song is not strictly a *blues*, it certainly has a blues feel to it. You can play "John Henry" using the two chords we have just learned, and most of the time you will simply stay with the A chord.

When it comes to changing chords, my good friend Pat Alger likes to talk about economy of motion. "Move your hands as little as possible," he tells students at guitar workshops, "and don't overshoot your mark." This is excellent advice. The movement back and forth from A to E should be easy and fluent, and you should use as little energy as possible.

John Henry

Your strumming hand should also move as little as possible. Many eager beginning guitarists flail the strings as though they were making an overhand smash in a tennis match. The sound produced is a nerve-jangling vibration of strings—like being in the wrong gear in a sports car. Your touch—the way your fingers hit the strings, the tone you produce, and the ease with which you play—will be very important later on. It's best to start correctly and play with a light, but firm touch.

Picking the Strings

Now that you know two chords—and the song "John Henry"—let's move on to some right-hand technique, known as picking or fingerpicking. There are many ways to approach fingerstyles with your right hand; from the country-folk picking made popular by Merle Travis and Chet Atkins, to the jazz-flavored styles of Earl Klugh and Charlie Byrd. Classical players also rely on a fluid right-hand style, so whatever your preference, you will have to learn fingerpicking to some extent.

I believe that right-hand technique begins and ends with the thumb. In fact, when a guitarist tells me he or she is all thumbs, I consider that good news. Your thumb should set the basic rhythm for any song you are playing, eventually bouncing from string to string on the bass notes.

Let's begin with your thumb plucking the fifth string while you fret an A chord. The fifth string is an A, so it is the *root* note of the chord. Lightly pluck down on the fifth string with your thumb, following with a brush downward across the other strings with your index finger, or the curled fingers of your right hand.

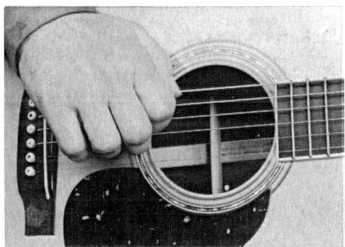

What you want to do is play a bass note with your thumb, then brush down . . . play another bass note, brush down again . . . bass note, brush down . . . etc. Rhythmically, it should look like this.

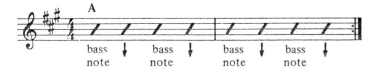

When you play this strum, try to sound like a smooth, Nashville-style, country-music picker. Take it slowly at first, gradually increasing the tempo.

Now try the same strum on an E chord. This time, hit the E (or sixth) string in the bass, to correspond with the *root* note of chord.

Once you have this basic strum down, you might try the alternating bass, that is, alternating between the fifth and sixth strings with your thumb.

Now try "John Henry" with a full strum. It should start sounding richer and fuller right away. We will come back to this strumming technique later, but now let's take a look at the third chord in the key of A, the D chord:

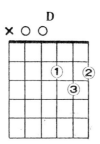

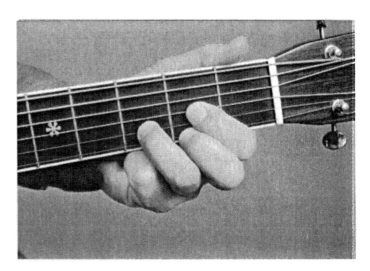

Now that you know the A, E, and D chords in the key of A, you will be able to play a wide variety of songs. In fact, most country-western, folk, and rock and roll songs use only three chords! Let's try a very well-known traditional song, "Will the Circle Be Unbroken." This tune has been played and recorded by scores of performers over the years. (Probably the most famous version is the title cut on the Nitty Gritty Dirt Band's best-selling album.)

Will the Circle Be Unbroken

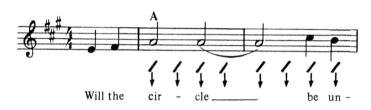

Once you can handle the chord changes easily and smoothly, try playing "Will the Circle Be Unbroken" with the alternating-bass strum you have just learned. Here's how it looks:

Will the Circle Be Unbroken

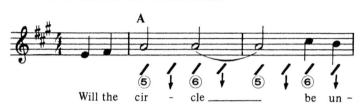

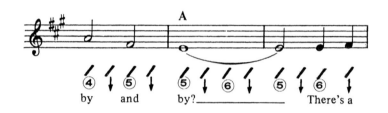

To Pick or Not to Pick: Flatpicks, Fingerpicks, and Thumbpicks

Many guitarists find that fingerpicks produce a crisper, brighter sound on their guitar, particularly with steel-string models. While this is certainly true, I would not recommend using them at this time, although you might want to get a set of them to see how they work. I used fingerpicks for many years, eventually discarding them so I could *feel* the strings with my fingertips and nails. This is an important consideration for the beginning guitarist, who will need his or her sense of touch to get rooted with the instrument.

Flatpicks are another story. They are generally made of plastic, although in the old days, guitarists loved the natural resilience of tortoise-shell picks. These turtles are now an endangered species, so don't bother looking for tortoise-shell picks these days. You should choose a few different flatpicks to fool around with. They are very inexpensive, which is good since they often get lost.

Picks come in hard, medium, and soft gauges. Buy one of each and see which feels best in your hands. I began playing with a very soft pick, since its pliability seemed to make playing easier for me. Eventually, I switched to hard picks because they produce a brighter, more rounded tone. It is simply a matter of personal choice.

Whether to use fingerpicks, flatpicks, or no picks at all, is a decision only you can make. Earl Klugh, an innovative jazz-style guitarist, does not use fingerpicks (although he has used a thumbpick) on his nylon-string guitar. Albert King, the legendary blues guitarist, plays everything with his bare thumb, still managing to get a percussive sound. Freddie King, on the other hand, uses a thumbpick and one fingerpick to alternate between strings. Andrés Segovia, of course, uses no picks for his classical playing. Eric Clapton, who plays many styles of guitar, generally uses a medium-gauge flatpick on his electric.

There is an incredible range of approaches to guitar playing. Some styles are more conducive to the use of picks. You'd be hard-pressed to find a bluegrass rhythm-guitarist without a flatpick in his or her hand. And most electric jazz-players use a flatpick as well. The legendary jazz guitarist Wes Montgomery once said that he developed his incredibly flexible thumb-style because "no one told me *not* to do it! I made my own way!" Eventually, you will have to make that choice for yourself. Like an abstract painter, you should learn the basics before making your own moves.

Now, let's return to "Will the Circle Be Unbroken" and play it using a flatpick. Hold the pick between your right thumb and index finger—not too tight, but not too loose either. You want to exert a fair amount of pressure without overdoing it.

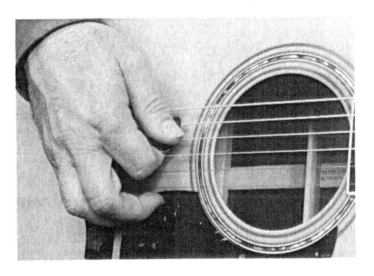

As you can see, only a small part of the pick should project beyond the edges of your thumb and finger. Your wrist should stay relaxed—to get the feeling, shake the pick as if you were shaking a thermometer.

Now, hit the fifth string while holding an A chord and strum down as you did before. Is the sound clean? Can you hear all of the notes? If the sound is muddy, don't despair. Pete Seeger once said that "playing guitar is as easy as walking—but it took us all a couple of years to learn how to walk!" You will get the hang of the pick eventually, if you keep at it.

Midnight Special

Here's another very popular folk song to try in the key of A. Notice that one chord is different. Instead of an E chord, we are going to use an E7 chord in this progression.

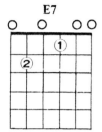

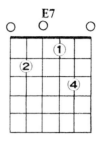

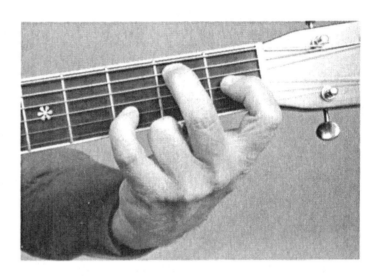

Midnight Special

Chord Study

Now that you have learned the basic chords in the key of A, let's take a look at some other chords. Many chords overlap from one key to another. The D and A chords, for example, are equally at home in the key of D and the key of A, and they show up in other keys as well. Let's look at three chords in the key of D:

G

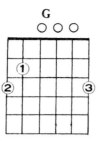

D

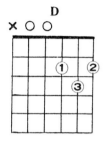

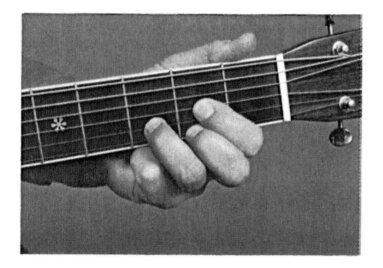

A7

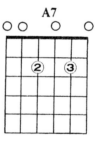

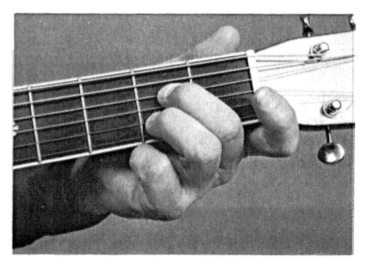

Now let's try a version of "Midnight Special" in the key of D.

Midnight Special

Notice that you must use different bass notes with each chord. "Frankie and Johnny" is another song that you can play in D. To *transpose* a song is to play it in a new key. Eventually, you should be able to transpose songs from one key to another with ease. The basic chords for the keys of C, E, and G are shown below.

BASIC CHORDS IN THE KEY OF C

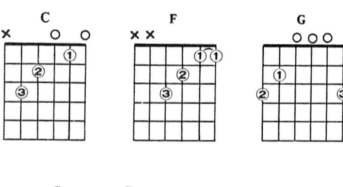

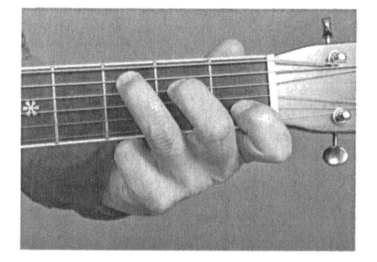

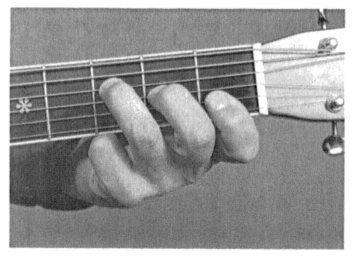

BASIC CHORDS IN THE KEY OF E

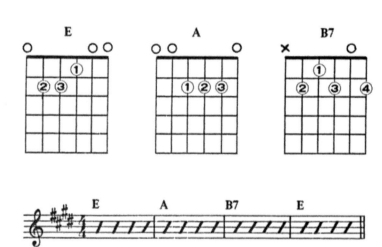

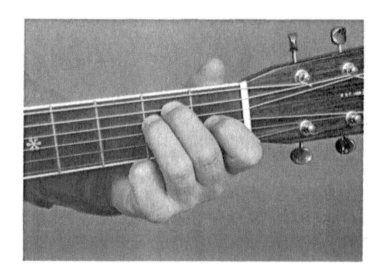

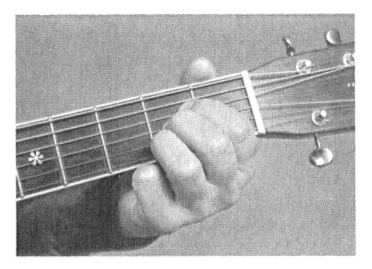

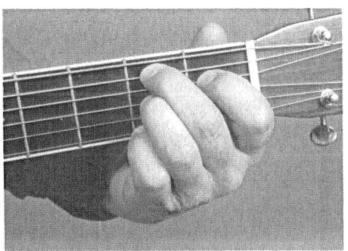

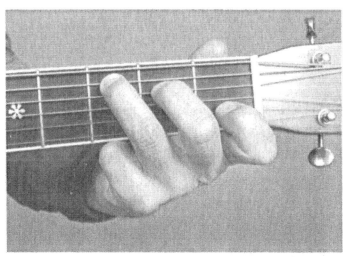

BASIC CHORDS IN THE KEY OF G

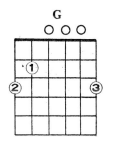 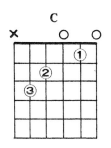 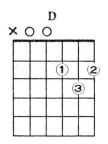

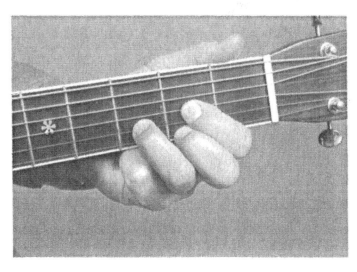

Single-String Techniques

Everybody wants to be a lead guitarist these days—playing finger-bending solos at breakneck speed. While that is an admirable goal to strive for, we can't all be Eddie Van Halen or George Benson overnight. The best we can do is to play gracefully and tastefully—at whatever level we may be. I'd like to start your single-string playing with a series of notes that relate to a G chord. Many instructors will start you with scales or finger exercises—but that seems static and boring to me. Below, you will find a series of diagrams, each of which represents a single note. Slowly, follow these notes down until you reach the last one. Then strum a G chord. This little *riff* will get your fingers roving from the top (first) string to the bottom (sixth) string.

At first, I would recommend using a flatpick to hit these notes. Use downstrokes on each one. Later, you will want to use upstrokes (V) and downstrokes (⋒) alternately.

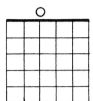
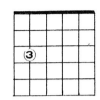

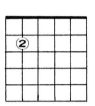
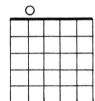

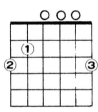

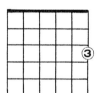
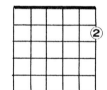
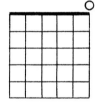

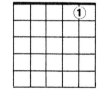
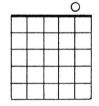

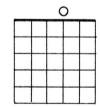

A Word About Guitar Tablature

"I think it's good to read music . . . but not necessarily for everybody. Ear training is really more important. I learned guitar mostly by ear."

Nancy Wilson of Heart

When reading tablature you will notice horizontal lines representing each of the strings on the guitar. The high E is on the top, and the other strings line up accordingly. Numbers placed on the lines indicate frets. The *riff* we just learned in the key of G looks like this in tablature.

Many guitarists cannot read a single note of music, and play, as they say 'by ear'. I would, however, suggest that you study musical notation at some point in your training. It can open many doors for you.

Further Chord Study

Mama Don't 'Low

Let's learn some more songs in different keys. To start with, let's try a bluegrass-style song called "Mama Don't 'Low." As you will see, this is the kind of song to which you can add your own verses. One of my favorite verses is: "Mama don't allow no guitar teachers around here!"

Mama Don't 'Low

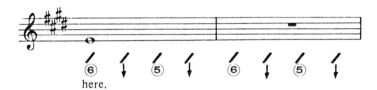

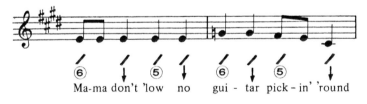

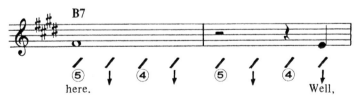

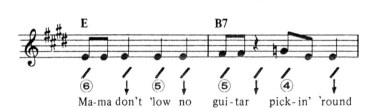

Crawdad

This next song, one of the first that I ever learned on guitar, is a natural in the key of E. Expand your strum on this song by going down (↓) and then up (↑) with the pick (or fingers). In other words, hit a bass note and then strum down/up immediately.

Crawdad

You get a line and I'll get a pole,— hon-ey.

You get a line and I'll get a pole,—

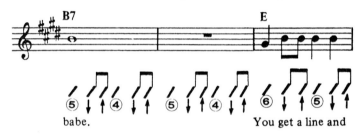

babe. You get a line and

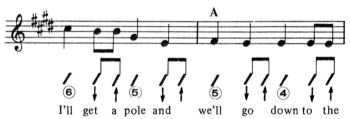

I'll get a pole and we'll go down to the

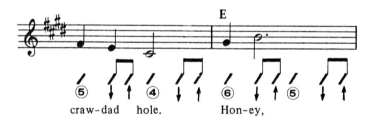

craw-dad hole. Hon-ey,

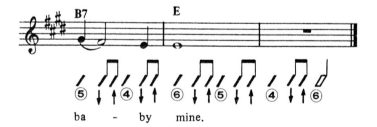

ba - by mine.

Minor Chords

Try these three new chords:

A minor

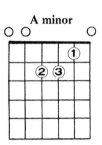

D minor

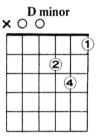

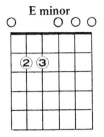

E minor

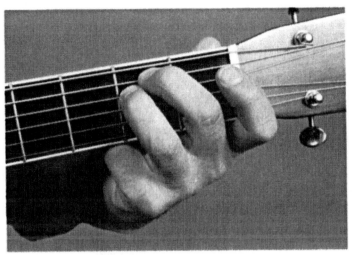

Using minor chords along with the chords you have already learned will open a whole new world of sound to you. For example:

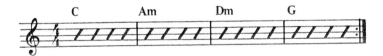

C   Am   Dm   G

This progression was used in countless rock and roll ballads througout the do-wop days of the 1950s. You might also want to try it in the key of G.

G   Em   Am   D

St. James Infirmary

Minor chords also work well in sad blues songs like this old standard, "St. James Infirmary." In a song of this type, I would suggest a slow series of rhythmic downstrokes, using your fingers or a flat-pick.

St. James Infirmary

Am   E7   Am

It was down in old Joe's bar-room,— on a

Dm   E7   Am   E7

cor-ner by— the square.— *etc.* The drinks were served as

Am   E7   Am

u-sual,— and the u-su-al crowd was there.

Now, let's put together a major and minor chord with a moving *bass run* to link them together. Starting with a G chord, hit the sixth string, strum down/up (⊓ V)—hit the sixth string at the 2nd fret (an F♯ note). Then hit the open sixth string (an E note) strumming on an E minor chord. It looks like this:

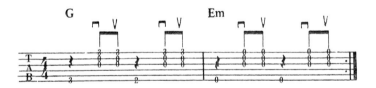

G   Em

Bass runs are very important in song accompaniment and add texture to your playing. You will get to the point where you can move your right hand quickly enough to play the bass run and to reach the next chord without losing the rhythm. Remember, your touch and tone are the most important parts of your playing, at whatever level. Always pay close attention to these aspects of your playing.

Fingerpicking: An Introduction

Fingerpicking is perhaps the most satisfying of all guitar styles, and it is one of the most difficult to master. There are endless ways to approach this technique: from the thumping blues of Robert Johnson, Skip James, and Ry Cooder, to the subtle melodic ideas of Doc Watson, Chet Atkins, and Eric Schoenberg. Fingerpicking can be incredibly complex, but all of it rests on a simple, solid foundation.

As I mentioned before, your thumb is the pivot point of all fingerpicking. Let's start with an A chord. Slowly move your thumb back and forth from the fifth string to the fourth string. Give one beat to each note.

Now, *pinch* the fifth string and the first string, using the thumb and index finger of your right hand. Follow that by bringing your thumb down to the fourth string.

Try the same idea using an E chord:

Now try a D chord:

This is the essence of fingerpicking. Later on, you may want to add your middle and ring fingers for more complex picking patterns, but for now you are well on your way. Remember to keep your thumb moving steadily in rhythm at all times.

Well, that brings us to the end of this introduction to the guitar. I hope my information has been helpful, interesting, and fun! The Bibliography will help you find books that will take you further in your study of the guitar. Don't give up! The world needs as many guitarists as it can get.

Chord Glossary

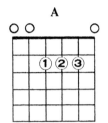
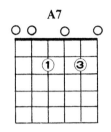
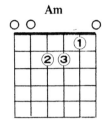
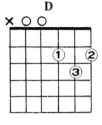
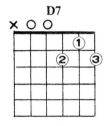
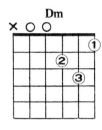

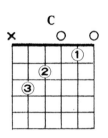
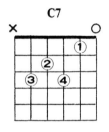
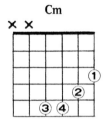
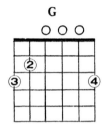
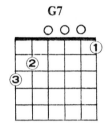
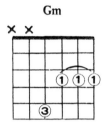

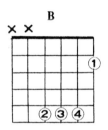
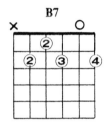
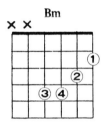
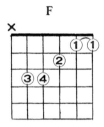
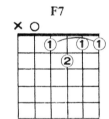
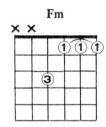

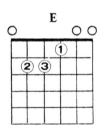
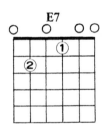
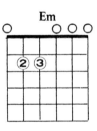

Bibliography

There are many excellent resources available as you continue your study of the guitar. Here are a few ideas to try after you have learned the chords and techniques presented in this book.

Homespun Tapes (Box 694, Woodstock, New York 12498) offers a wide selection of guitar instruction on audio and video cassettes. My own series, **Rock Guitar** and **Beginning Jazz,** are available, as well as other tapes. Write for catalogue.

The Guitarist's Picture Chord Encyclopedia by John Pearse (Music Sales Corporation) features every chord a guitarist will ever need.

There are other books in Music Sales' **Picture Chords** series, including my **Jazz Picture Chords and How to Use Them.** I would recommend this to students who wish to move ahead on the guitar, whether or not they are interested in jazz.

How to Play Blues Guitar by Arlen Roth (Music Sales Corporation) offers an easygoing approach to basic chords, rhythms, and styles of the blues.

Improvising Rock Guitar by Arti Funaro and Artie Traum (Music Sales Corporation) is a more advanced study of the playing styles of Jimi Hendrix, Eric Clapton, and others.

Fingerpicking Styles for Guitar by Happy Traum (Music Sales Corporation) offers the sixteen most important fingerpicking techniques for guitar students.

There are scores of books available for guitarists, and obviously it would be impossible to list them all here. A careful glance at your local music store will reveal a world of written, taped, and filmed materials to help you progress.

STEP ONE:

Guitar
for Beginners

Book Two: Chords

Amsco Publications
A Part of **The Music Sales Group**
New York/London/Paris/Sydney/Copenhagen/Berlin/Tokyo/Madrid

CD Track List

Contents

Chord Construction

Scales

In order to talk about chord structure we need to discuss the foundation by which chords are formed—*scales*. There are a multitude of scales available to the musician, but we will explain only those that are most pertinent—the major, minor, and chromatic scales.

Major

Harmonic minor

Melodic minor

Chromatic

Scales are determined by the distribution of *half steps* and *whole steps*. For example, the major scale has half steps between scale steps three and four, and between seven and eight. The harmonic minor has half steps between scale steps two and three, five and six, and seven and eight. The melodic minor scale's ascending order finds half steps between scale steps two and three, and between seven and eight. Descending, the half steps fall between scale steps six and five, and between three and two; and a whole step is now in place between eight and seven.

It is common to refer to scale steps, or *degrees,* by Roman numerals as in the example above and also by the following names:

    I. Tonic
   II. Supertonic
  III. Mediant
  IV. Subdominant
   V. Dominant
  VI. Submediant
 VII. Leading tone

Intervals

An *interval* is the distance between two notes. This is the basis for harmony (chords). The naming of intervals, as in the example below, is fairly standard, but you may encounter other terminology in various forms of musical literature.

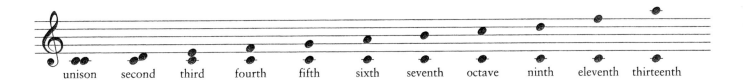

unison   second   third   fourth   fifth   sixth   seventh   octave   ninth   eleventh   thirteenth

Chords

Chords are produced by combining two or more intervals, and the simplest of these combinations is a *triad.* A triad consists of three notes obtained by the superposition of two thirds. The notes are called the *root,* the *third,* and the *fifth.*

Inversions

Inversions are produced by arranging the intervals of a chord in a different order. A triad that has the root as the bottom or lowest tone is said to be in *root position*. A triad with a third as the bottom or lowest tone is in *first inversion,* and a triad with a fifth as the bottom or lowest tone is in *second inversion.* As the chords become more complex—such as, sixths, sevenths, etc.—there will be more possible inversions.

root   first inversion   second inversion

Note that when inverting more complex chords the inversion may actually become a completely different chord.

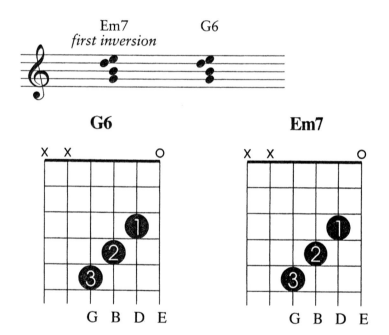

Altered Triads

When a chord consists of a root, major third, and a perfect fifth it is known as a *major triad.* When the triad is altered by lowering the major third one half-step, it becomes a *minor triad.* The examples below are chords that have altered intervals.

How to Use This Book

The Chord Diagram

The chords are displayed as diagrams that represent the fingerboard of the guitar. There are six vertical lines representing the six strings of the guitar. Horizontal lines represent the frets. The strings are arranged with the high E (first, or thinnest) string to the right, and the low E (sixth, or thickest) to the left. The black circles indicate at which fret the finger is to be placed and the number tells you which finger to use. At the top of the diagram there is a thick black line indicating the nut of the guitar. Diagrams for chords up the neck just have a fret line at the top with a Roman numeral to the right to identify the first fret of the diagram. Above the chord diagram you will occasionally see x's and o's. An x indicates that the string below it is either not played or damped, an o simply means the string is played as an open string. At the bottom of the diagram are the note names that make up the chord. This information can be helpful when making up lead licks or chord solos. A curved line tells you to bar the strings with the finger shown; that is, lay your finger flat across the indicated strings.

The fingerings in this book might be different from fingerings you have encountered in other chord books. They were chosen for their overall practicality in the majority of situations.

The Photo

The photo to right of each chord diagram shows you what your hand should look like on the guitar fingerboard. You will notice that the finger positions in some of the photos are a little to the right or left of the frame. This is done to show the particular chord form's proximity to either the twelfth fret or the nut of the guitar. This makes it easier to recognize the relative position on the fretboard at a glance.

Although the photos are a visual reference, all of the fingers in a given shot may not be in a proper playing position. We have sometimes moved unused fingers *out of the way*, to give you a better look at where the fretting fingers are placed. For instance, when playing the Absus4 shown in the photograph below, your second and third finger should not be tucked under the neck, they would be relaxed and extended upward over the fingerboard. Make sure your fingers are comfortable and that you are capable of moving them easily from one chord position to another.

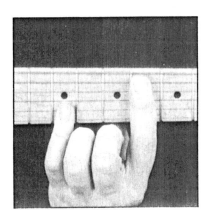

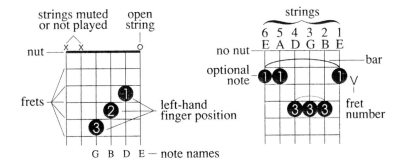

7

C chords

C major

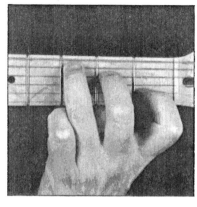

(o)   o   o

① ② ③

E C E G C E

C major

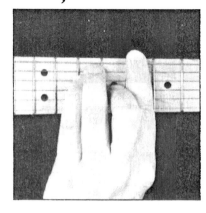

① ① ① VIII
②
③ ④

C G C E G C

Csus4

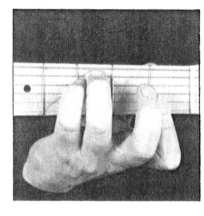

x   o

① ①
③ ④

C F G C F

C6

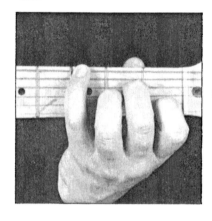

x   x

①
② ③
④

G   E A C

C7

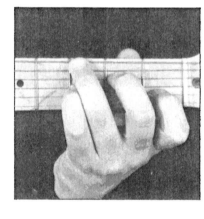

o

①
②
③ ③ ④

G C E B♭ C E

C°7

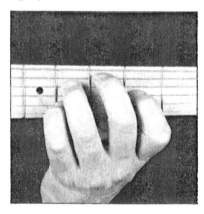

x   x

①
②
③ ④

C G♭ B♭♭ E♭

C9

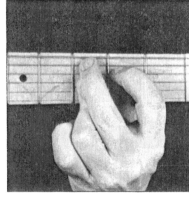

x

①
② ③ ③ ③

C E B♭ D G

C13

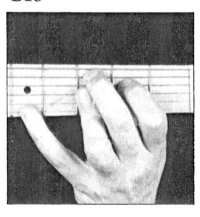

x

①
② ③ ③
④

C E B♭ D A

8

Cmaj7

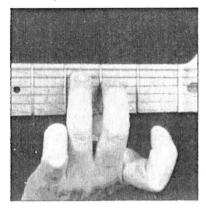 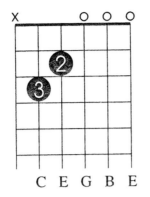

C E G B E

Cm7

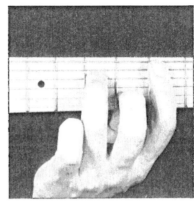 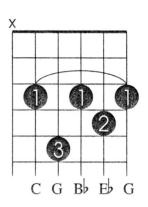

C G Bb Eb G

Cm

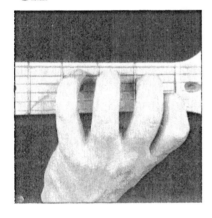 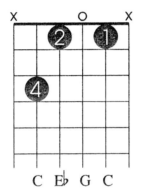

C Eb G C

Cm

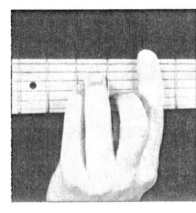 

G C G C Eb G

Cm6

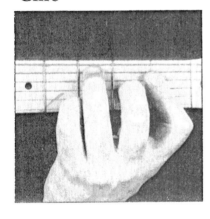 

C Eb A C G

Cm7b5

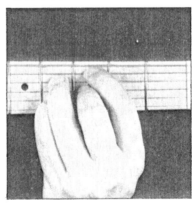 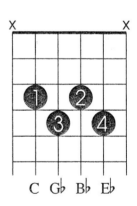

C Gb Bb Eb

Cm(maj7)

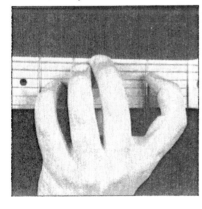 

G C Eb B

Cm11

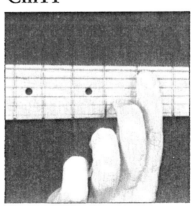 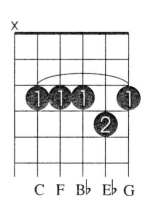

C F Bb Eb G

9

C#/Db chords

C# major

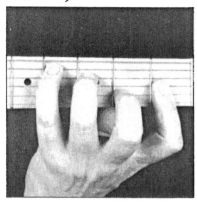

X

C# E# G# C# E#

C# major

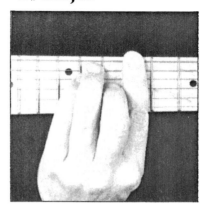

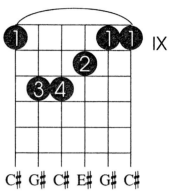

IX

C# G# C# E# G# C#

C#sus4

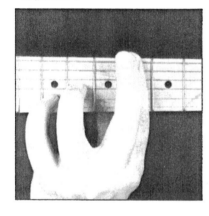

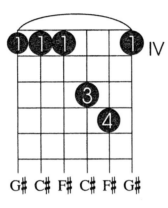

IV

G# C# F# C# F# G#

C#6

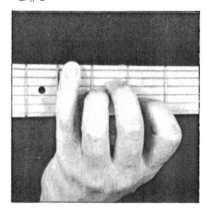

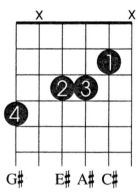

X   X

G#   E# A# C#

C#7

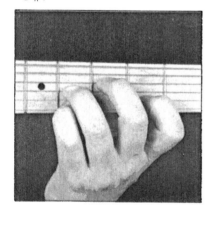

X X

E# B C# G#

C#°7

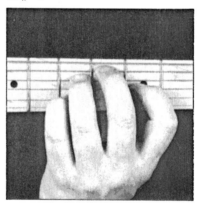

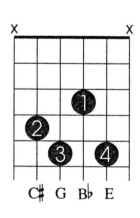

X   X

C# G Bb E

C#9

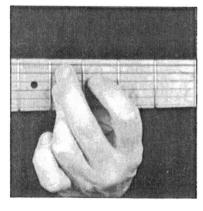

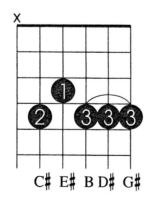

X

C# E# B D# G#

C#13

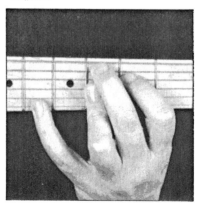

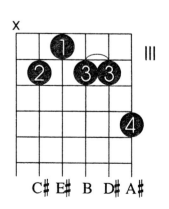

X

III

C# E# B D# A#

C#maj7

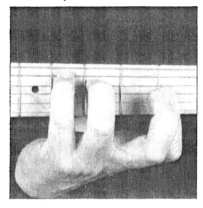
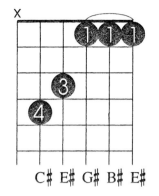

x

C# E G# B# E#

C#m7

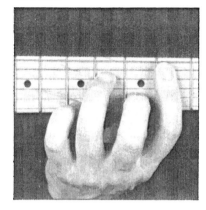
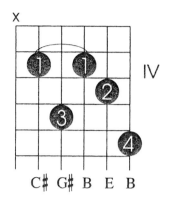

x

IV

C# G# B E B

C#m

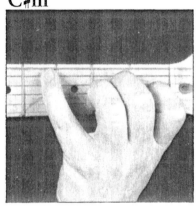

x   x

C# E G# C#

C#m

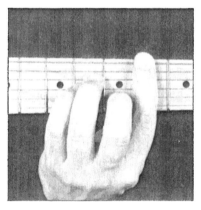
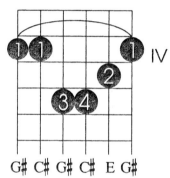

IV

G# C# G# C# E G#

C#m6

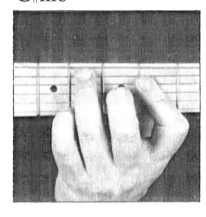
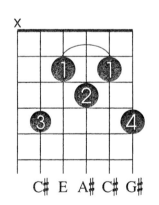

x

C# E A# C# G#

C#m7b5

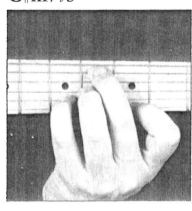

x   x

C#   B E G

C#m(maj7)

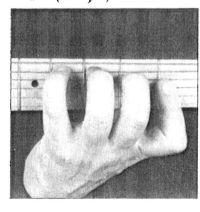
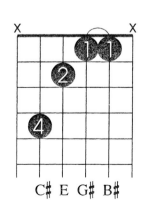

x   x

C# E G# B#

C#m11

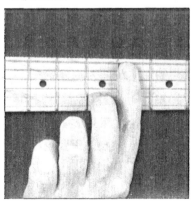
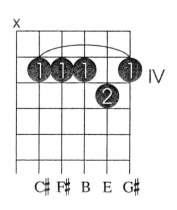

x

IV

C# F# B E G#

D chords

D major

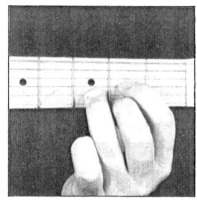

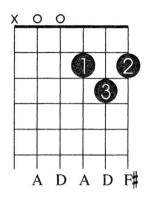

x o o

A D A D F#

D major

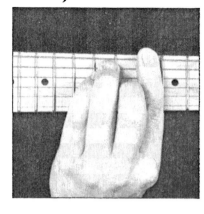

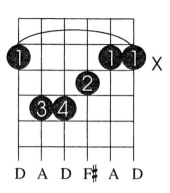

X

D A D F# A D

Dsus4

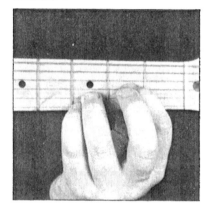

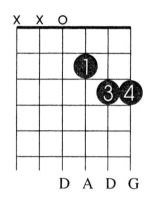

x x o

D A D G

D6

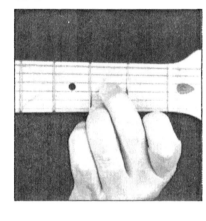

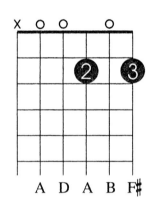

x o o o

A D A B F#

D7

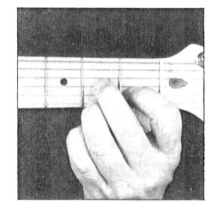

x o o

A D A C F#

D°7

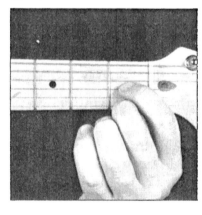

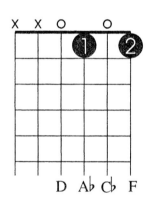

x x o o

D Ab Cb F

D9

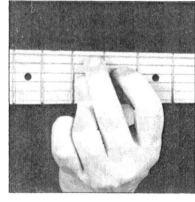

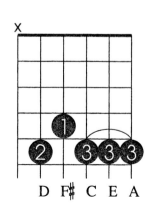

x

D F# C E A

D13

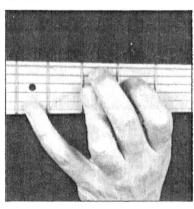

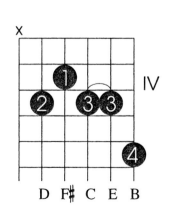

x

IV

D F# C E B

Dmaj7

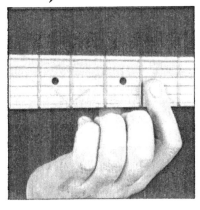
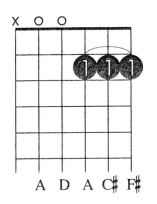

A D A C# F#

Dm7

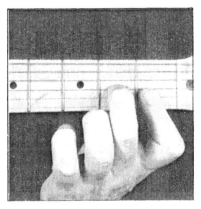

D A C F

Dm

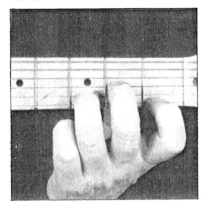
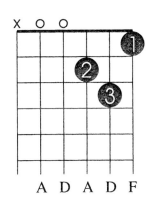

A D A D F

Dm

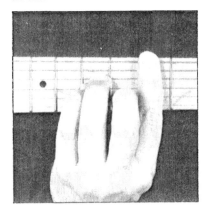
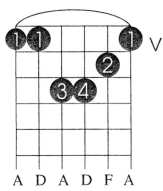

A D A D F A

Dm6

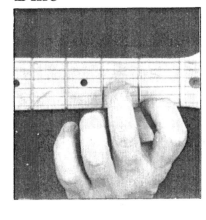

D A B F

Dm7♭5

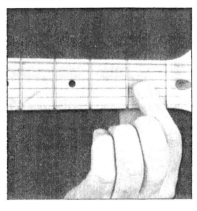
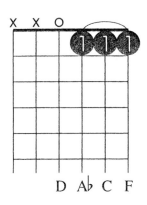

D A♭ C F

Dm(maj7)

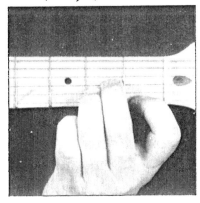
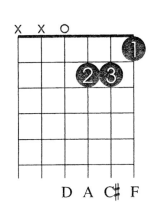

D A C# F

Dm11

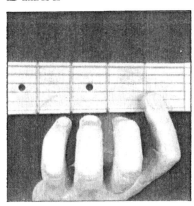
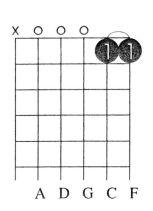

A D G C F

E♭/D♯ chords

E♭ major

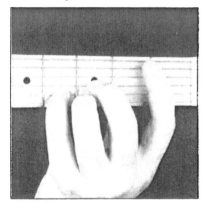

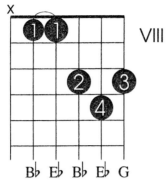

X
① ①
② ③
④

VIII

B♭ E♭ B♭ E♭ G

E♭ major

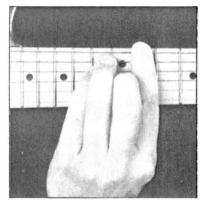

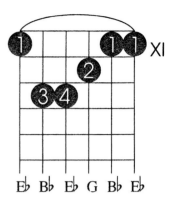

① ① ①
②
③ ④

XI

E♭ B♭ E♭ G B♭ E♭

E♭sus4

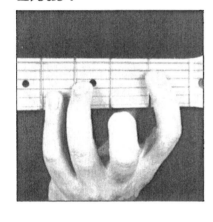

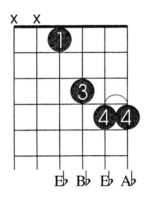

X X
①
③
④ ④

E♭ B♭ E♭ A♭

E♭6

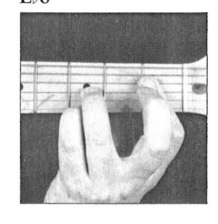

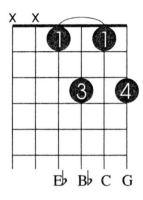

X X
① ①
③ ④

E♭ B♭ C G

E♭7

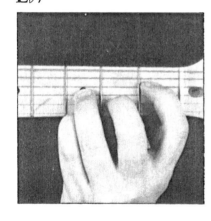

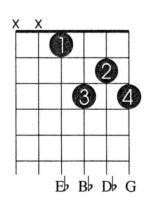

X X
①
②
③ ④

E♭ B♭ D♭ G

E♭°7

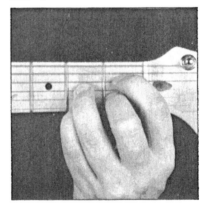

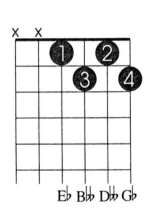

X X
① ②
③ ④

E♭ B♭♭ D♭♭ G♭

E♭9

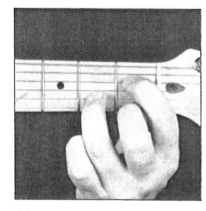

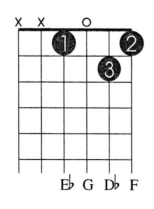

X X O
① ②
③

E♭ G D♭ F

E♭13

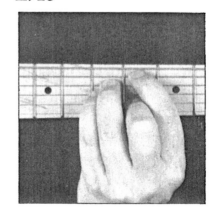

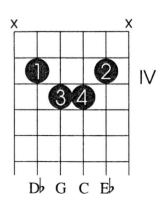

X X
① ②
③ ④

IV

D♭ G C E♭

E♭maj7

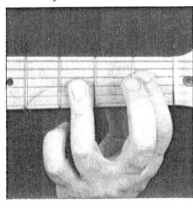
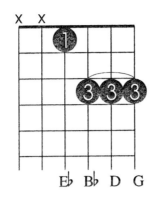

X X

①
③ ③ ③

E♭ B♭ D G

E♭m7

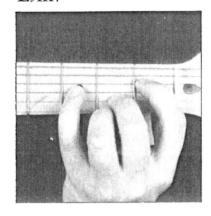
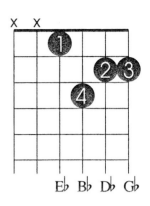

X X

①
② ③
④

E♭ B♭ D♭ G♭

E♭m

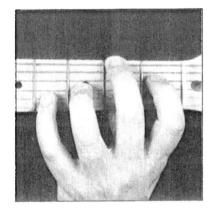

X X

② ①
③
④

G♭ E♭ B♭ E♭

E♭m

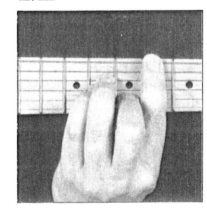
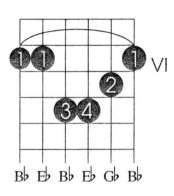

① ① ①
②
③ ④

VI

B♭ E♭ B♭ E♭ G♭ B♭

E♭m6

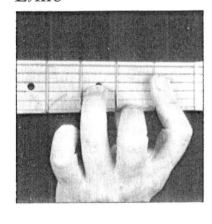
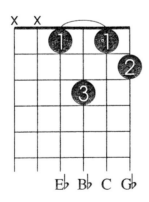

X X

① ①
②
③

E♭ B♭ C G♭

E♭m7♭5

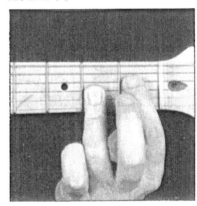
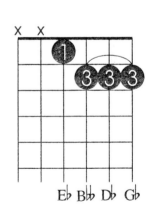

X X

①
③ ③ ③

E♭ B♭♭ D♭ G♭

E♭m(maj7)

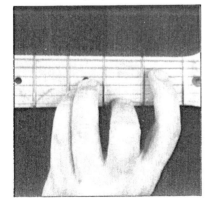
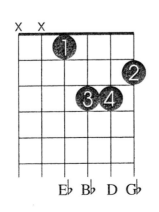

X X

①
②
③ ④

E♭ B♭ D G♭

E♭m11

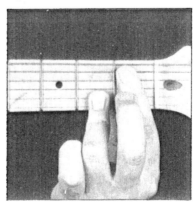
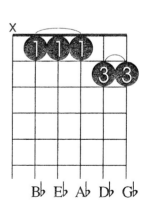

X

① ① ①
③ ③

B♭ E♭ A♭ D♭ G♭

15

E chords

E major

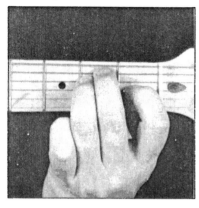
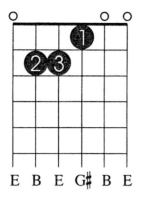

E B E G# B E

E major

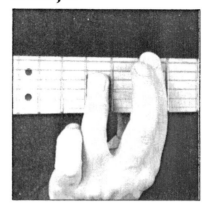
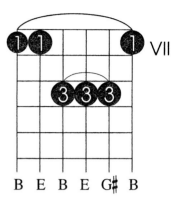

VII

B E B E G# B

Esus4

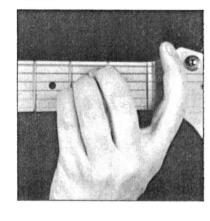
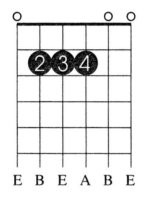

E B E A B E

E6

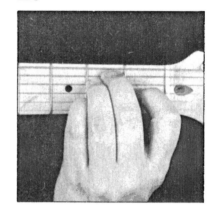
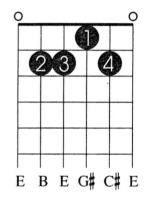

E B E G# C# E

E7

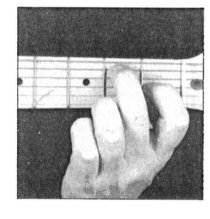
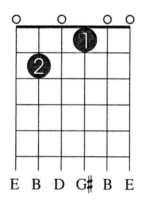

E B D G# B E

E°7

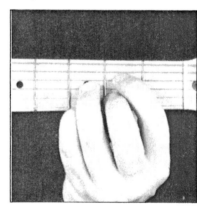
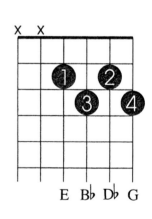

E B♭ D♭ G

E9

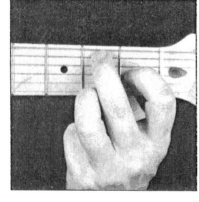
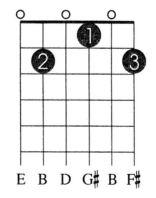

E B D G# B F#

E13

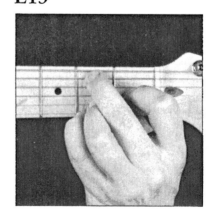
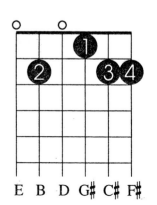

E B D G# C# F#

Emaj7

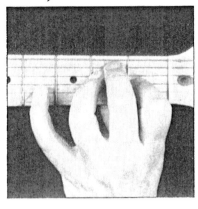
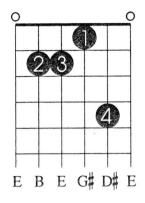

E B E G# D# E

Em7

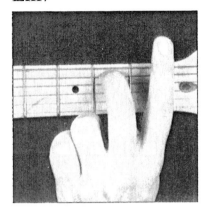
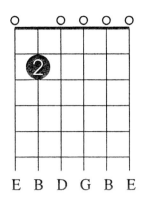

E B D G B E

Em

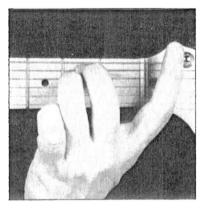
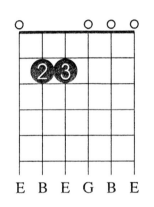

E B E G B E

Em

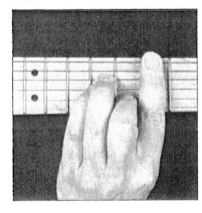
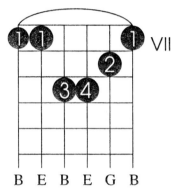

VII

B E B E G B

Em6

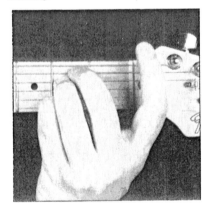

E B E G C# E

Em7b5

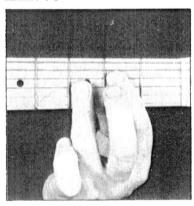
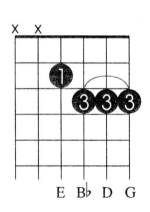

x x

E Bb D G

Em(maj7)

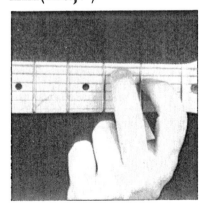
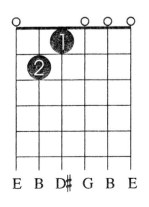

E B D# G B E

Em11

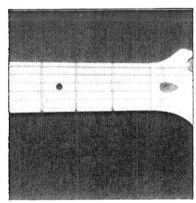
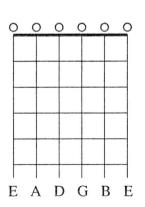

E A D G B E

F chords

F major

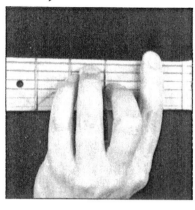
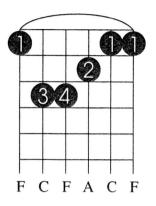

F C F A C F

F major

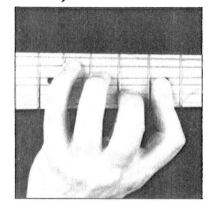
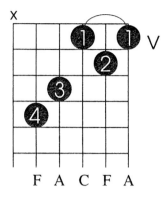

x

V

F A C F A

Fsus4

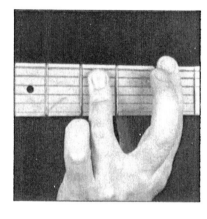

F C F B♭ C F

F6

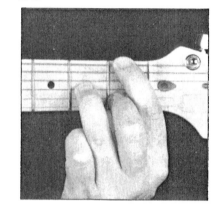
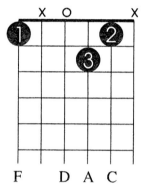

x O x

F D A C

F7

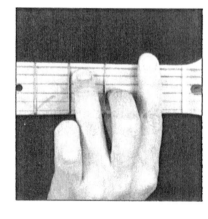
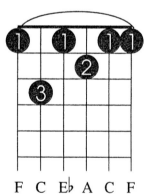

F C E♭ A C F

F°7

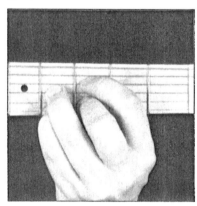
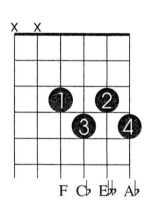

x x

F C♭ E♭♭ A♭

F9

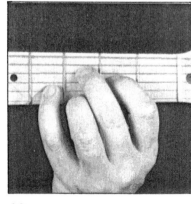
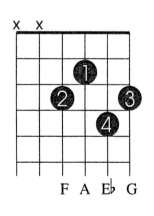

x x

F A E♭ G

F13

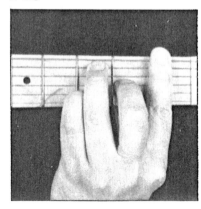

F C E♭ A D F

Fmaj7

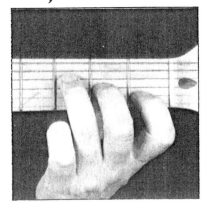 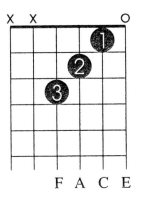

X X O

F A C E

Fm7

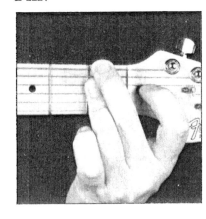 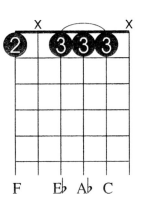

X X

F Eb Ab C

Fm

F C F Ab C F

Fm

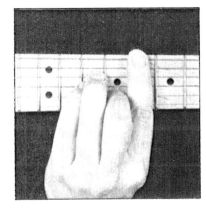 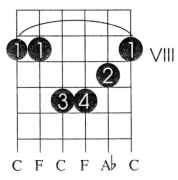

VIII

C F C F Ab C

Fm6

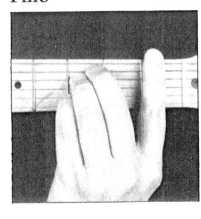 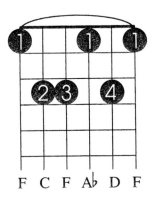

F C F Ab D F

Fm7b5

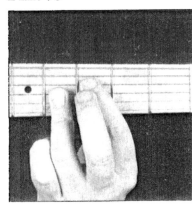 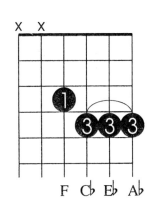

X X

F Cb Eb Ab

Fm(maj7)

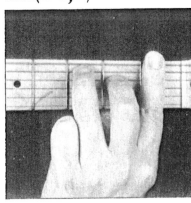 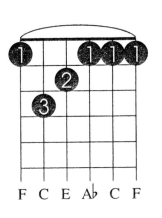

F C E Ab C F

Fm11

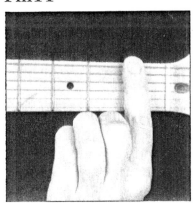 

F Bb Eb Ab C F

F#/Gb chords

F# major

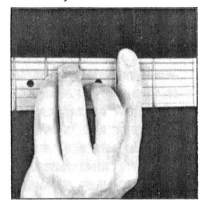

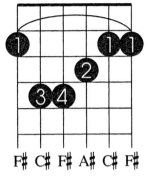

F# C# F# A# C# F#

F# major

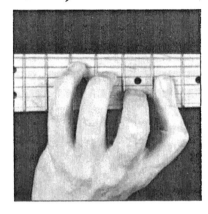

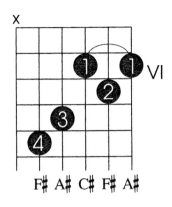

x

VI

F# A# C# F# A#

F#sus4

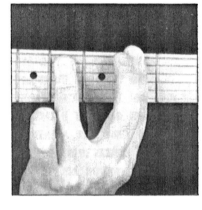

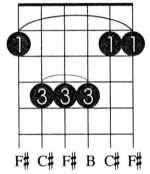

F# C# F# B C# F#

F#6

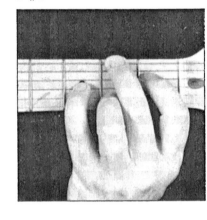

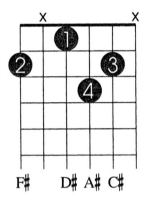

x   x

F#   D# A# C#

F#7

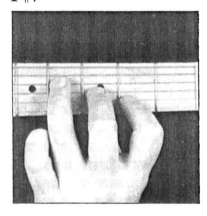

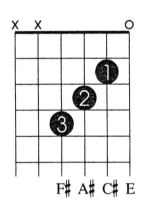

x x   o

F# A# C# E

F#°7

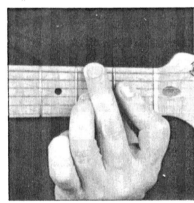

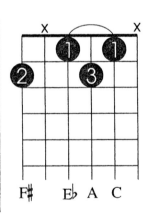

x   x

F#   Eb A C

F#9

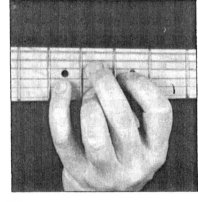

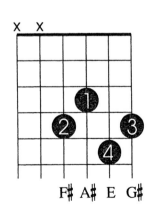

x x

F# A# E G#

F#13

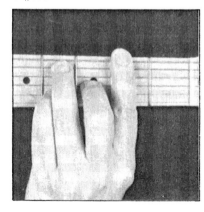

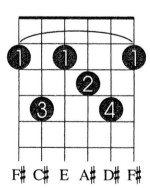

F# C# E A# D# F#

F#maj7

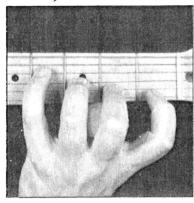

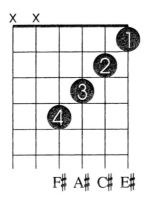

X X

1
2
3
4

F# A# C# E#

F#m7

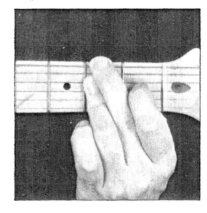

X X

2 3 3 3

F# E A C#

F#m

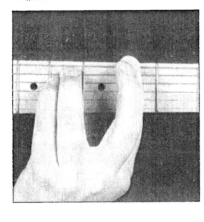

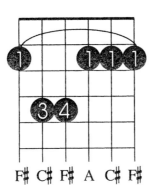

1 1 1 1

3 4

F# C# F# A C# F#

F#m

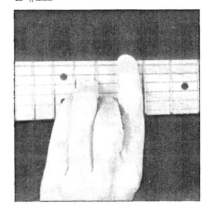

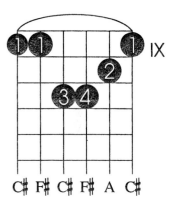

1 1 1 IX
2
3 4

C# F# C# F# A C#

F#m6

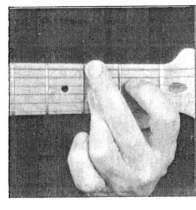

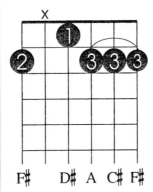

X

1
2 3 3 3

F# D# A C# F#

F#m7b5

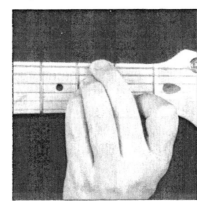

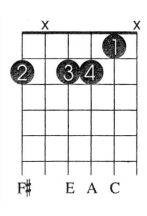

X X

1
2 3 4

F# E A C

F#m(maj7)

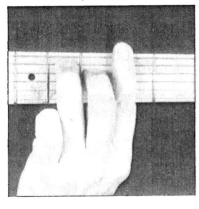

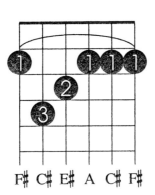

1 1 1 1
2
3

F# C# E# A C# F#

F#m11

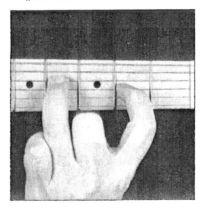

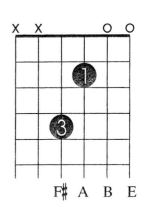

X X O O

1

3

F# A B E

21

G chords

G major

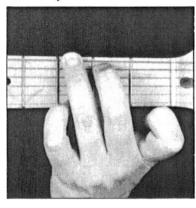

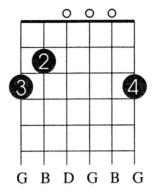

G B D G B G

G major

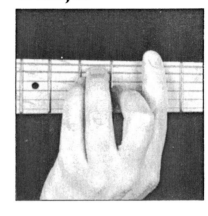

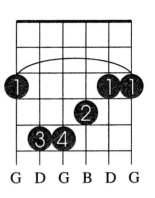

G D G B D G

Gsus4

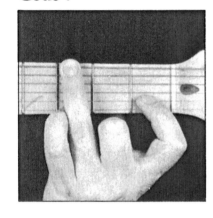

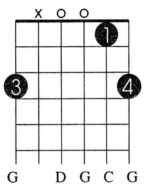

G D G C G

G6

G B D G B E

G7

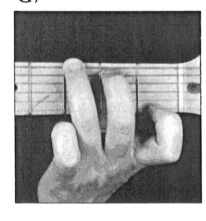

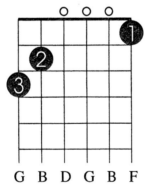

G B D G B F

G°7

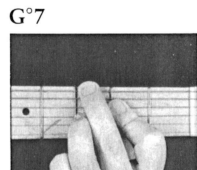

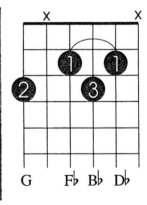

G Fb Bb Db

G9

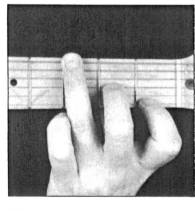

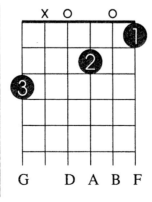

G D A B F

G13

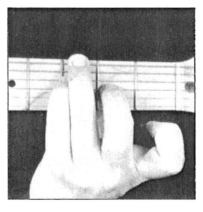

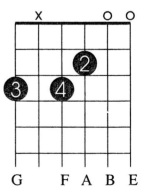

G F A B E

Gmaj7

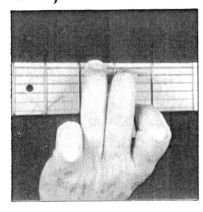
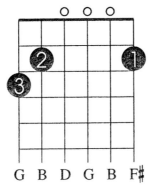

G B D G B F#

Gm7

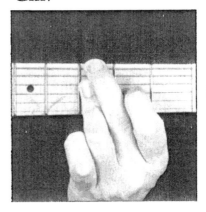
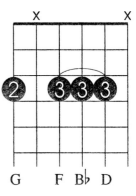

G F Bb D

Gm

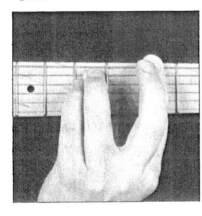
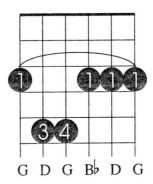

G D G Bb D G

Gm

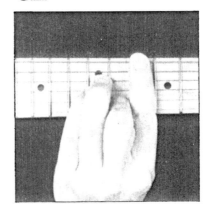
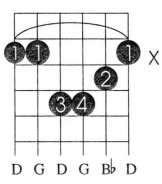

D G D G Bb D

Gm6

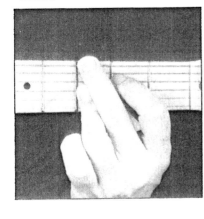
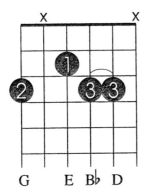

G E Bb D

Gm7b5

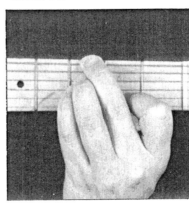
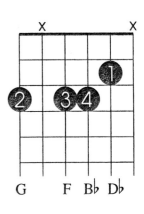

G F Bb Db

Gm(maj7)

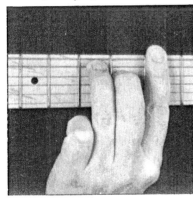
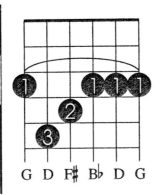

G D F# Bb D G

Gm11

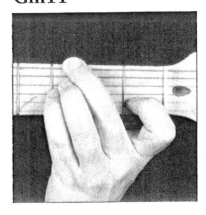
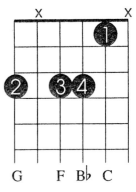

G F Bb C

A♭/G♯ chords

A♭ major

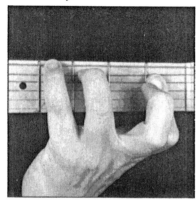

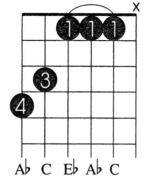

A♭ C E♭ A♭ C x

A♭ major

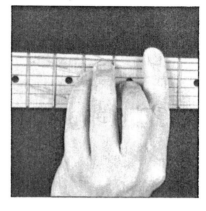

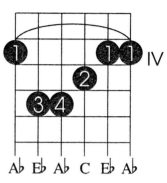

A♭ E♭ A♭ C E♭ A♭ IV

A♭sus4

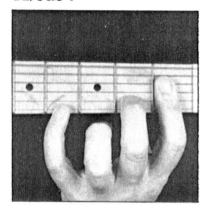

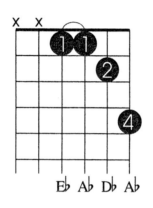

x x
E♭ A♭ D♭ A♭

A♭6

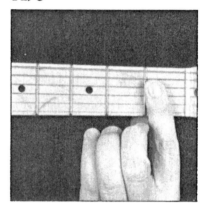

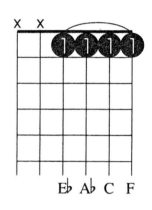

x x
E♭ A♭ C F

A♭7

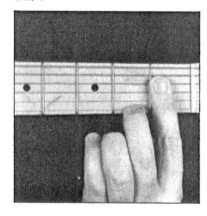

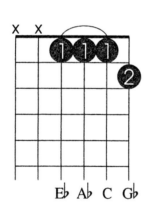

x x
E♭ A♭ C G♭

A♭°7

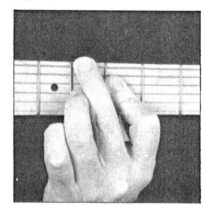

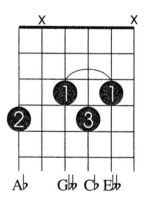

x   x
A♭   G♭♭ C♭ E♭♭

A♭9

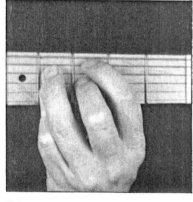

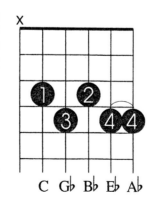

x
C G♭ B♭ E♭ A♭

A♭13

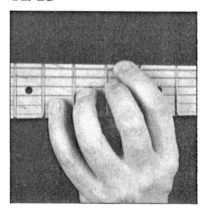

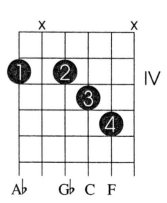

x   x
A♭   G♭ C F IV

A♭maj7

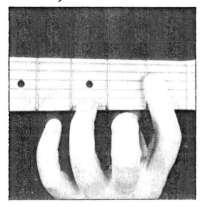
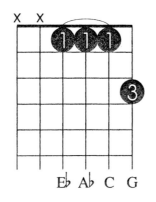

E♭ A♭ C G

A♭m7

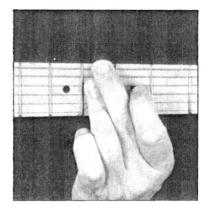
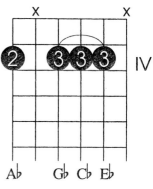

IV

A♭ G♭ C♭ E♭

A♭m

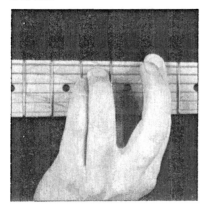
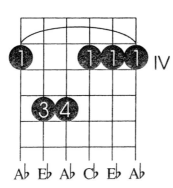

IV

A♭ E♭ A♭ C♭ E♭ A♭

A♭m

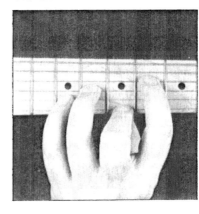
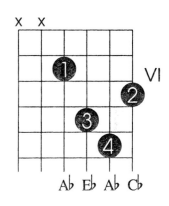

VI

A♭ E♭ A♭ C♭

A♭m6

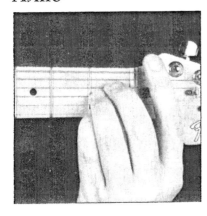
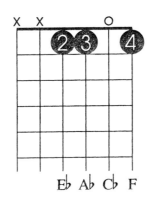

E♭ A♭ C♭ F

A♭m7♭5

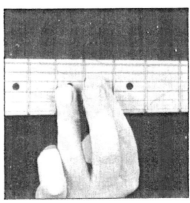
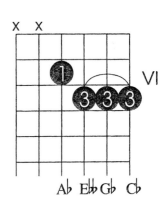

VI

A♭ E♭♭ G♭ C♭

A♭m(maj7)

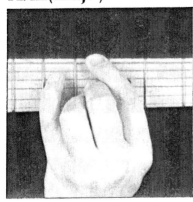
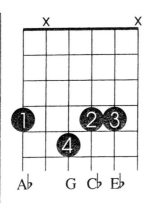

A♭ G C♭ E♭

A♭m11

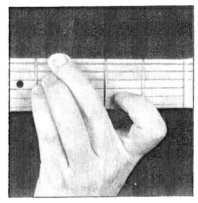

A♭ G♭ C♭ D♭

A chords

A major

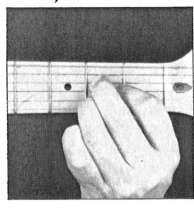
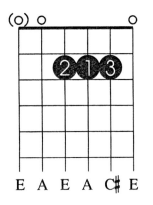

(o) o   o   o

② ① ③

E A E A C♯ E

A major

①   ① ① V

②

③ ④

A E A C♯ E A

Asus4

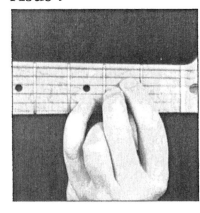

(o) o   o

① ②

④

E A E A D E

A6

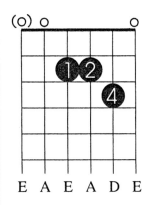

(o) o

① ① ① ①

E A E A C♯ F♯

A7

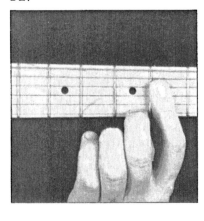

(o) o

① ① ①

②

E A E A C♯ G

A°7

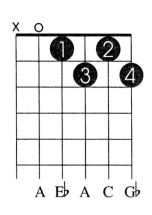

x   o

①   ②

③   ④

A E♭ A C G♭

A9

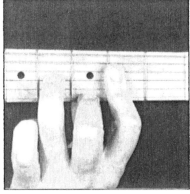

x o

① ① ①

②

③

A E B C♯ G

A13

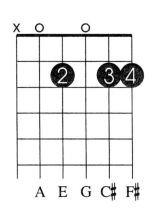

x o   o

②   ③④

A E G C♯ F♯

26

Amaj7

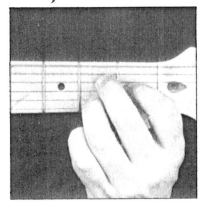 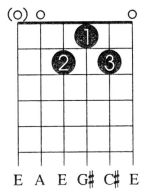

E A E G# C# E

Am7

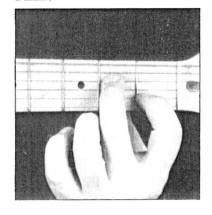 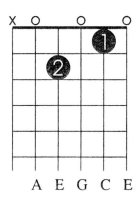

A E G C E

Am

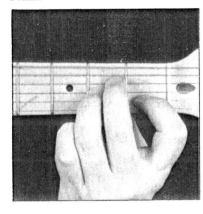 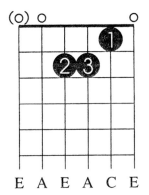

E A E A C E

Am

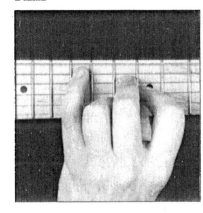 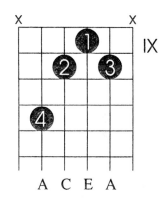

IX

A C E A

Am6

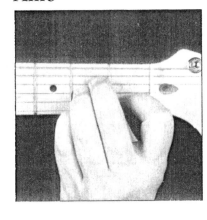 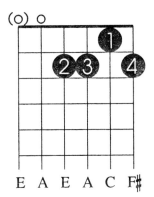

E A E A C F#

Am7♭5

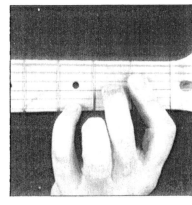 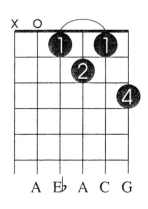

A E♭ A C G

Am(maj7)

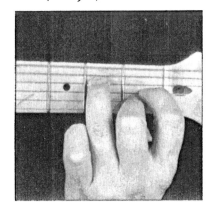 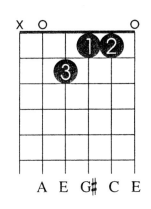

A E G# C E

Am11

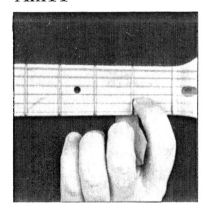 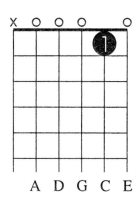

A D G C E

Bb/A# chords

Bb major

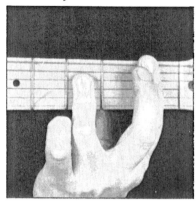

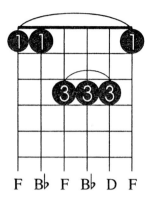

F Bb F Bb D F

Bb major

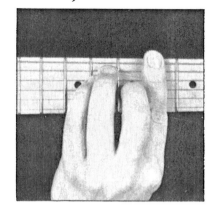

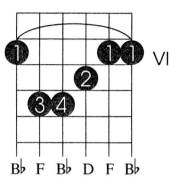

VI

Bb F Bb D F Bb

Bbsus4

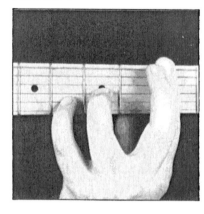

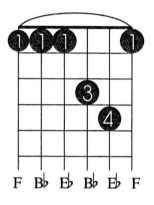

F Bb Eb Bb Eb F

Bb6

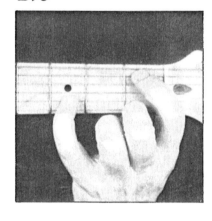

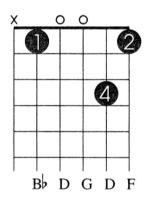

Bb D G D F

Bb7

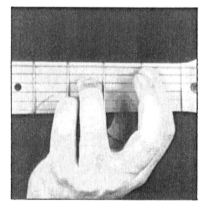

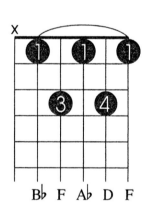

Bb F Ab D F

Bb°7

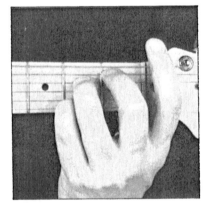

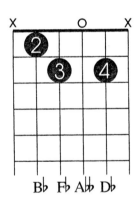

Bb Fb Abb Db

Bb9

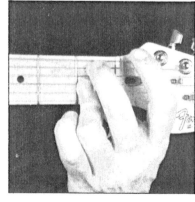

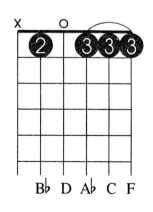

Bb D Ab C F

Bb13

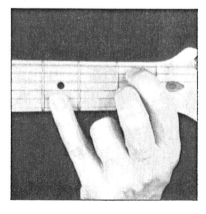

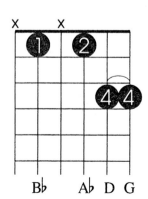

Bb Ab D G

B♭maj7

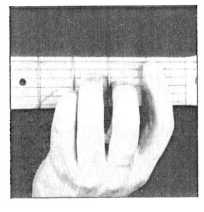

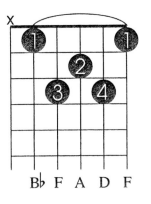

B♭ F A D F

B♭m7

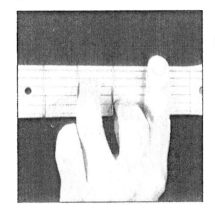

F B♭ F A♭ D♭ F

B♭m

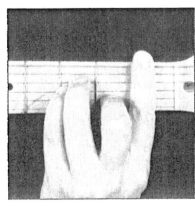

F B♭ F B♭ D♭ F

B♭m

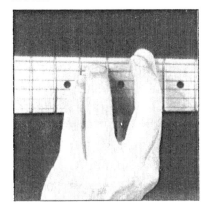

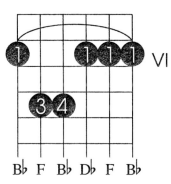

VI

B♭ F B♭ D♭ F B♭

B♭m6

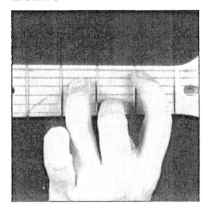

B♭ F G D♭

B♭m7♭5

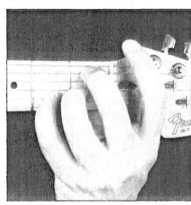

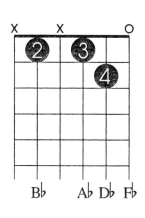

B♭ A♭ D♭ F♭

B♭m(maj7)

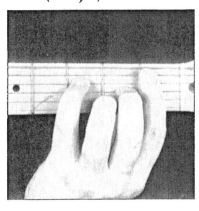

B♭ F A D♭ F

B♭m11

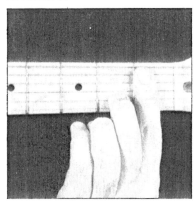

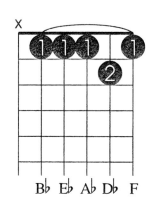

B♭ E♭ A♭ D♭ F

29

B chords

B major

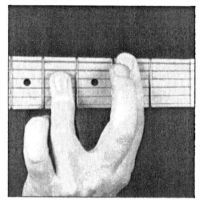
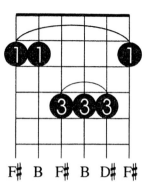

F# B F# B D# F#

B major

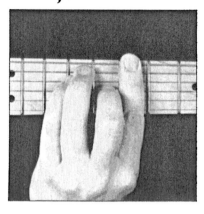
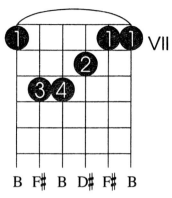

VII

B F# B D# F# B

Bsus4

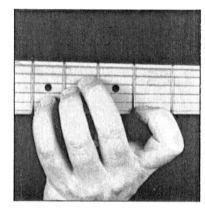
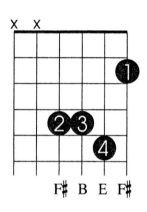

x x

F# B E F#

B6

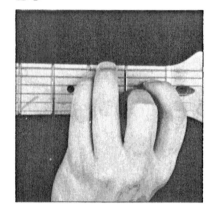
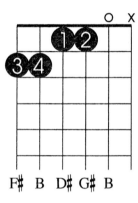

O x

F# B D# G# B

B7

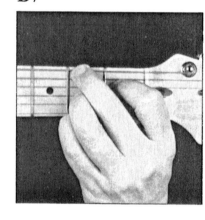
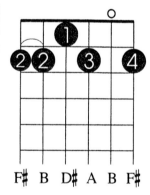

O

F# B D# A B F#

B°7

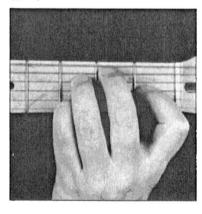
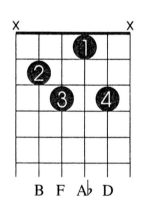

x x

B F Ab D

B9

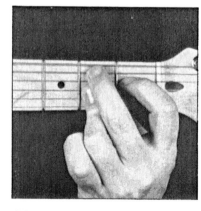
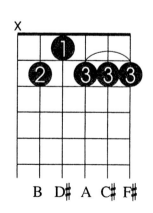

x

B D# A C# F#

B13

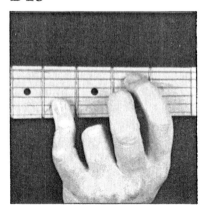
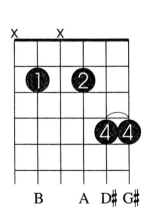

x x

B A D# G#

Bmaj7

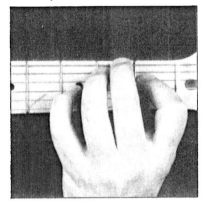
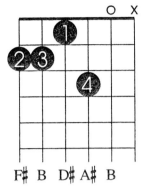

F# B D# A# B

Bm7

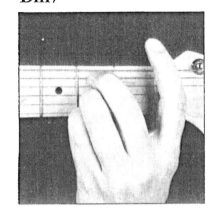

B D A B F#

Bm

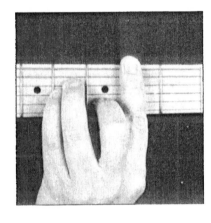
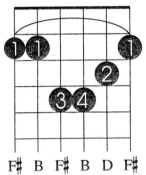

F# B F# B D F#

Bm

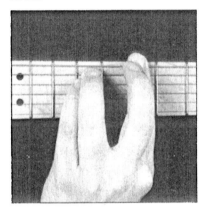
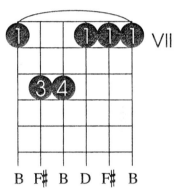

VII

B F# B D F# B

Bm6

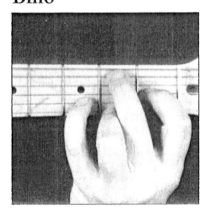
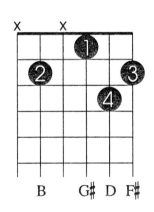

B G# D F#

Bm7b5

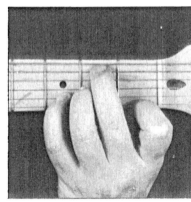
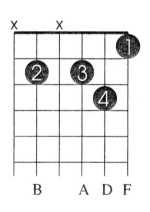

B A D F

Bm(maj7)

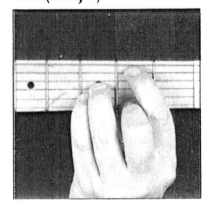
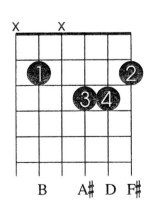

B A# D F#

Bm11

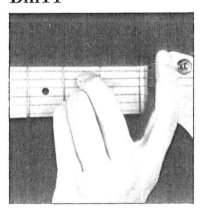

B D A C# E

Special Chords

The chords forms below are know as *5 chords* or *power chords*. These forms are most commonly used in rock, but you will find uses for them in other styles as well.

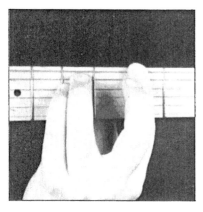 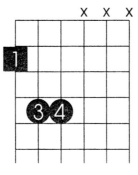

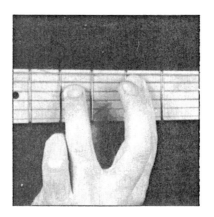 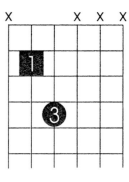

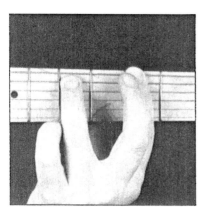 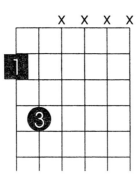

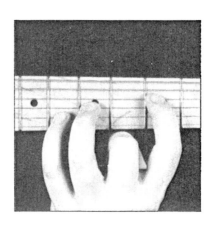 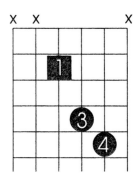

These forms are major and minor triads constructed on the first three strings.

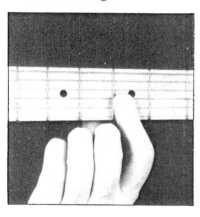 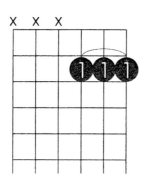

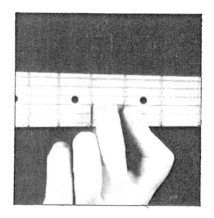 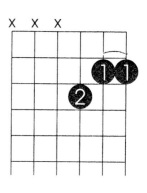

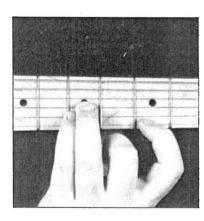 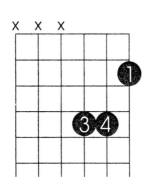

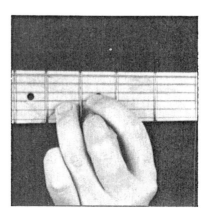 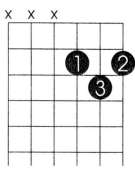

STEP ONE:

Guitar
for Beginners

Book Three: Scales

Amsco Publications
A Part of **The Music Sales Group**
New York/London/Paris/Sydney/Copenhagen/Berlin/Tokyo/Madrid

CD Track List

Contents

What Scales Can Do for You

Everybody who plays an instrument knows that practicing scales is important. But many guitarists, especially those of you who are self taught, do not get the benefit that they could from their scales either because they practice without any regularity or organized methodology, or, worse, because they practice scales without fully understanding them. Working with scales can do wonders for your playing, but they are not in and of themselves any kind of shortcut to "superchops." To really get the most out of scale practice, you must understand how different types of scales are constructed, the theory behind those constructions, as well as the best fingerings for different situations. Armed with these tools, an organized program of scale practice can not only provide you with technical facility and fingerboard familiarity, but also with theoretical understanding of tonal and chordal structures and their applications and, consequently, broadened improvising and even composing skills.

The more scales you are truly familiar with, the more choices you have available to you to use in building riffs for a set part or on the spur of the moment in a solo. Your way is also smoother when coming up with more extended melodies or harmony parts if you are confident of your knowledge of scale construction. Even your comping skills are enhanced as you are able to realize new embellishments for standard chords.

How to Use This Book

In the sections that follow, you will find basic explanations of scale theory and application. This material is designed to be general in nature and so it may apply to just about any style of contemporary music. In fact, it is often difficult to generalize about matters of style and genre when discussing musical building blocks as elemental as scales. Just because a scale is categorized as a "jazz" scale for the purposes of this book should not be taken to mean that it never turns up in rock or country or even polka music. On the other hand, if you regularly feature these so-called jazz scales in a more-or-less idiomatic way, your playing will tend to sound more-or-less jazzy.

No matter what your area of musical interest, you should attempt to master and practice all of the scale patterns outlined in the "Scales" section of the book. A few of the scales included are admittedly of limited musical use. Others may seem to have little relevance to the type of music you play. This is no reason to shy away, because practicing these scales may be considered to be technique practice in its purest form. Even if there appears to be little value in a three octave chromatic or diminished scale, smaller patterns contained within such a scale could crop up in just about any type of musical situation.

If you already have a routine for practicing scales, you may want to use this book simply as a thesaurus of scale forms and practice patterns. Even if you are thoroughly familiar with all of the forms presented, you will find that having all of them together in one source helps you to organize your practice sessions, allowing you to concentrate on the technical and musical aspects of the business at hand.

If you are not already versed in scale practice, pay special attention to the section "How to Practice Scales." Develop your personal routine and stick to it. If you cannot avail yourself of the advice of a good teacher, talk to guitar players you admire; in fact, talk to any guitar players you can. Another good source for ideas and advice is to be found in the many interviews with well-known guitarists, columns, and articles in magazines such as *Guitar Player, Guitar for the Practicing Musician,* and *Guitar World.* These magazines provide a wealth of supplemental theory and technique material every month in addition to some entertaining features.

Scale Theory

Simply defined, a scale is a series of tones organized according to a specific arrangement of *intervals*. An interval is the distance between any two tones, or pitches. The smallest interval (excepting the *unison*) is the *half step*, which corresponds to the difference in pitch between two notes one fret apart on the same string.

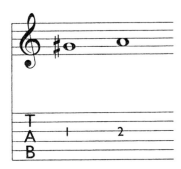

A distance of two half-steps is, naturally, a *whole step*.

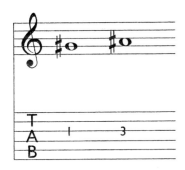

Any scale may be defined exclusively by its arrangement of whole and half steps. If you know a scale's formula of whole and half steps, you can construct that scale beginning on any note. For example, examine the layout of the major scale below.

C major scale (⌣ = whole step ⌣ = half step)

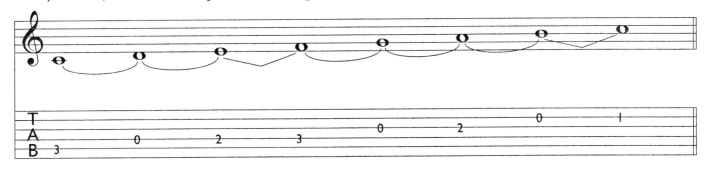

The formula of whole-whole-half-whole-whole-whole-half is the same for any major scale.

Major Scales and Key Signatures

If you look at the C major scale above in two halves, you can see that each half has the same formula of whole and half steps—that is, whole-whole-half—and that the two halves are separated by one whole-step. From what you know about scale formulas, this means that the second half of the C major scale can start off a new major scale. Since this new scale will begin on G, it is said to have a *tonal center* of G, or, more simply, to be a G major scale.

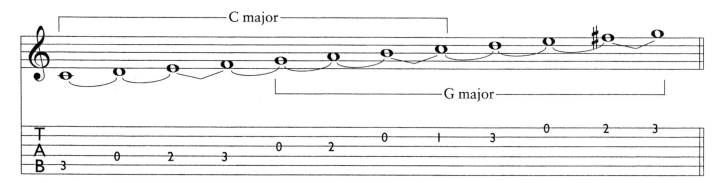

Notice that to keep the arrangement of whole and half steps the same as it was in the C major scale, the seventh degree of the G major scale must be sharped. Since the formula must be consistent, the G major scale will always contain an F♯. Because the scale always contains an F♯, the *key signature* of the key of G major is written like this:

Let's now take the second half of the G scale and use it as the first half of a new major scale. Notice that we have dropped the G major scale down an octave to put the new scale in a more easily playable range.

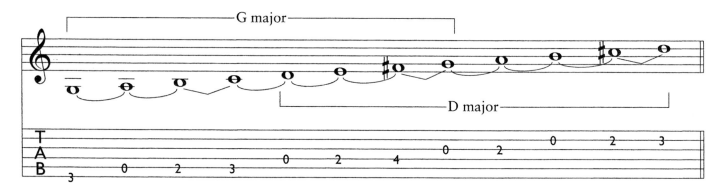

In the same way that the F♯ was added to the G scale, a C♯ must be added to the D scale to make it agree with the major scale formula. This means that the key signature of D major contains two sharps, F and C.

Continuing this process of taking the second half of a major scale to be the first half of the next will produce twelve distinct major scales each with its own distinct key signature. Notice that it is necessary to use flats rather than sharps to produce the scales in the second column of the following chart.

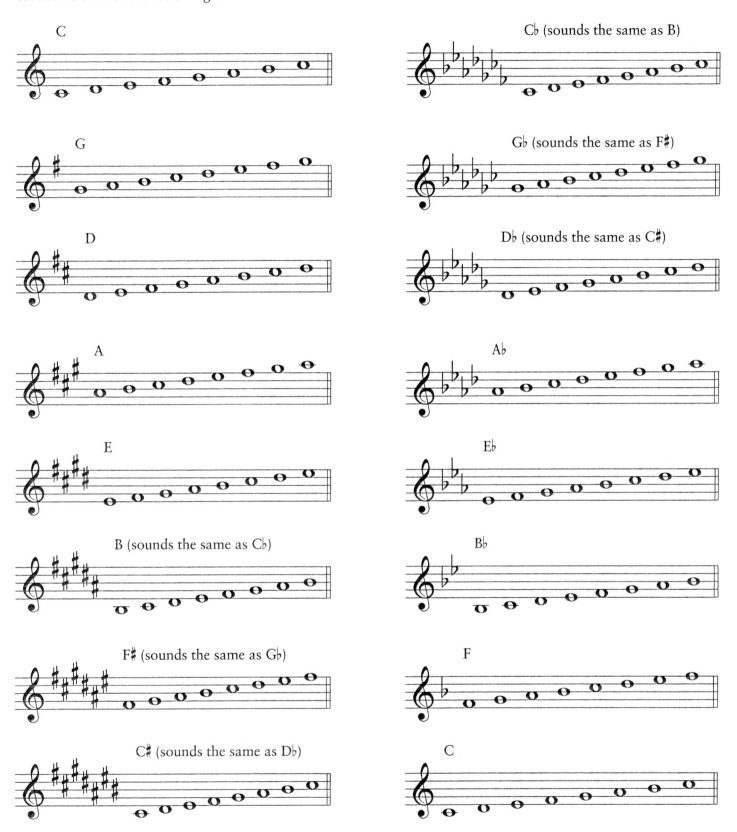

Although it is not necessary to memorize any of the foregoing material in order to make use of the scales and exercises in this book, having this information at your fingertips—as well as any other music theory you can pick up—can only help your playing.

The Circle of Fifths

The order in which the scales are presented in the chart above is referred to as the *circle of fifths*. It is a circle because it starts and ends at the key of C. It is the circle of fifths because each scale begins on the fifth degree of its preceding scale, or the interval of a perfect fifth above. This relationship of the twelve major scales may be expressed in the following circle diagram.

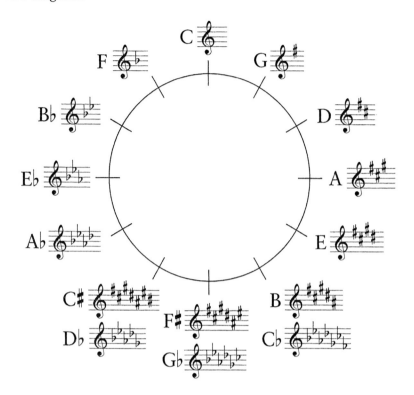

Minor Scales

Every one of the major scales has a corresponding *relative minor* scale that shares the same key signature. You can find the starting note of a major scale's relative minor scale by going up to the sixth degree of that major scale. Thus, the relative minor of C major is A minor.

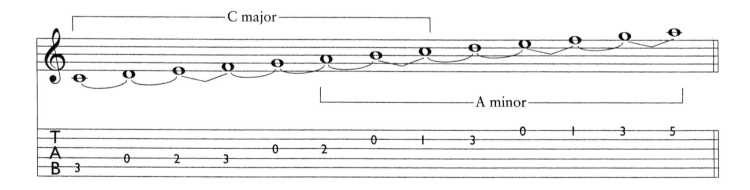

Here is a chart showing all of the relative minor scales.

Major Key	Relative Minor
C Major (no sharps or flats)	A Minor
G Major (one sharp: F♯)	E Minor
D Major (two sharps: F♯, C♯)	B Minor
A Major (three sharps: F♯, C♯, G♯)	F-sharp Minor
E Major (four sharps: F♯, C♯, G♯, D♯)	C-sharp Minor
B Major (five sharps: F♯, C♯, G♯, D♯, A♯)	G-sharp Minor
F-sharp Major (six sharps: F♯, C♯, G♯, D♯, A♯, E♯)	D-sharp Minor
C-sharp Major (seven sharps: F♯, C♯, G♯, D♯, A♯, E♯, B♯)	A-sharp Minor
F Major (one flat: B♭)	D Minor
B-flat Major (two flats: B♭, E♭)	G Minor
E-flat Major (three flats: B♭, E♭, A♭)	C Minor
A-flat Major (four flats: B♭, E♭, A♭, D♭)	F Minor
D-flat Major (five flats: B♭, E♭, A♭, D♭, G♭)	B-flat Minor
G-flat Major (six flats: B♭, E♭, A♭, D♭, G♭, C♭)	E-flat Minor
C-flat Major (seven flats: B♭, E♭, A♭, D♭, G♭, C♭, F♭)	A-flat Minor

Harmonic and Melodic Minor Scales

The relative minor scales referred to above are known as *natural minor* scales because they occur naturally, without deviating from their key signatures. These scales are commonly altered to form *harmonic minor* and *melodic minor* scales. The harmonic minor scale is formed by raising the seventh degree of a natural minor.

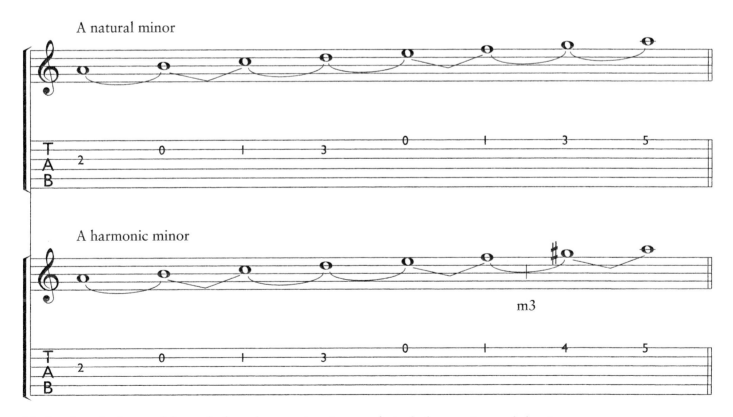

Notice that the interval formula for a harmonic minor scale includes one interval that is neither a whole step nor a half step. The *minor third*, abbreviated *m3*, is equal to three half-steps.

The other common type of minor scale is the *melodic minor* scale, produced by raising the sixth and seventh degrees of the natural minor scale.

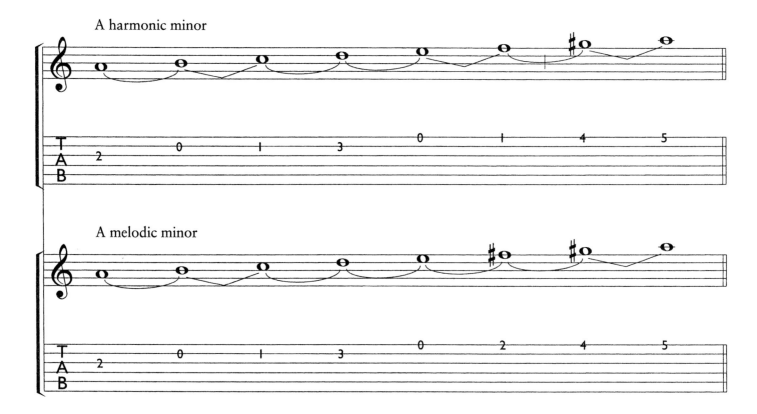

A harmonic minor

A melodic minor

Notice that the second half of the interval formula of a melodic minor scale is identical to that of a major scale. In fact, the only difference between a melodic minor scale and a major scale is the third degree.

Traditionally, the melodic minor scale form is said to follow the formula of the natural minor when descending.

A melodic minor

In recent times, it has become theoretically preferable to retain the same formula descending as ascending. Most people who think of the melodic minor in this way refer to it as a *jazz melodic minor* to distinguish it from the traditional interpretation. You will only find forms for the traditional melodic minor presented in the pages that follow, but you may easily practice jazz melodic minors by simply applying the same fingering going down as you do going up.

Modes

Modes are produced by displacing the starting point of a scale without changing its interval formula. This has the effect of turning out a scale with a new arrangement of whole and half steps. Most often, when musicians talk about modes they are referring to the seven modes of the major scale, although modes may be generated from any scale at all.

The modes are known by their Greek names (which were given to them by some rather creative Medieval theoreticians and have very little to do with Greece or Greek music).

The Dorian Mode

Starting on the second degree of a major scale yields a *Dorian* scale. This scale is very useful in jazz and jazz/rock—in which it is used for soloing over minor seventh chords—and sounds like the natural minor with a raised sixth.

D Dorian

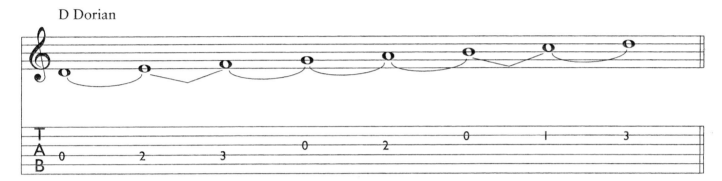

The Phrygian Mode

Playing a C major from E to E gives us an E *Phrygian* scale; reminiscent of flamenco music and sounding like the natural minor with a flatted second.

E Phrygian

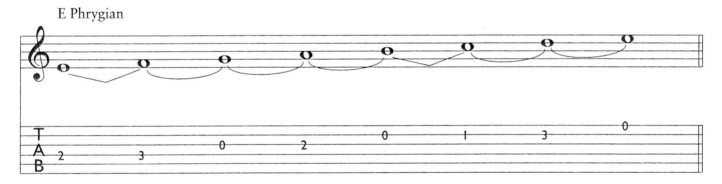

The Lydian Mode

The mode starting on the fourth degree of the major scale is known as a *Lydian* scale. This one has a major sound but differs from a straight major scale in its sharped fourth. In jazz, Lydian mode scales are generally used for soloing over major seventh chords other than the I chord.

F Lydian

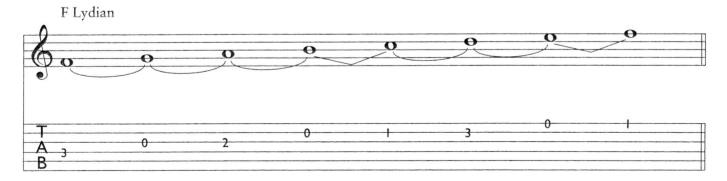

The Mixolydian Mode

Starting on the fifth degree of a major scale produces another major-sounding scale, the *Mixolydian* mode; this time with a flatted seventh. You will hear this one a lot in folk and rock music.

G Mixolydian

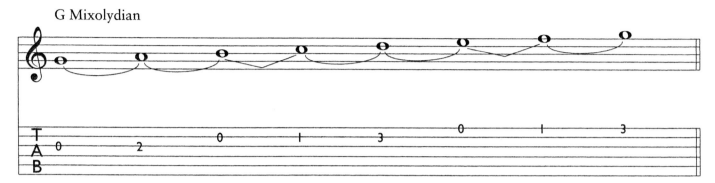

The Aeolian Mode

Remember that starting on the sixth degree of a major scale produces its relative minor. In the terminology of the modes, major is called *Ionian* and natural minor, *Aeolian*.

The Locrian Mode

The seventh mode, *Locrian,* was avoided for centuries due to its truly weird flavor. Because the scale outlines a diminished chord, melodies written in the Locrian mode never seem to quite come to rest. Inasmuch as this is sometimes a desirable quality in modern music, this mode has come into its own during the twentieth century. Also, the Locrian is useful in jazz soloing where it is commonly used over minor seventh flat-five (half-diminished) chords.

B Locrian

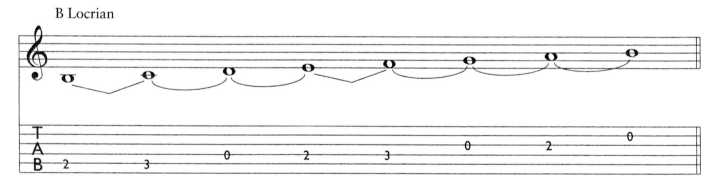

Chromatic Scales

A *chromatic* scale is the simplest example of a type of scale known as a *symmetrical* scale. The formula for a chromatic scale is simply all half steps.

Chromatic scale

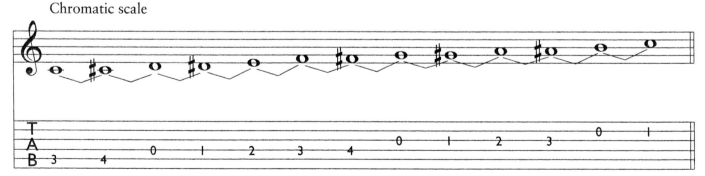

Because the intervals between notes are all identical, any note in the scale may be considered its root: no matter where you start, the formula will come out the same.

The chromatic scale is not really used as a scale for improvising (unless you consider that every melody is made up of notes from the chromatic scale—but that is not a very useful point of view). Since every type of music uses chromatic passages from time to time, the various patterns for this scale are well worth practicing.

Rock Scales

Major Pentatonic Scales

In addition to the usual major, minor, and modal scales, much rock music is based on five-note scales called *pentatonic* scales. The basic form of pentatonic scale is the major pentatonic built from the first, second, third, fifth, and sixth degrees of a major scale. This scale is often heard in Southern rock, rhythm and blues, country music, and light rock.

C major pentatonic scale

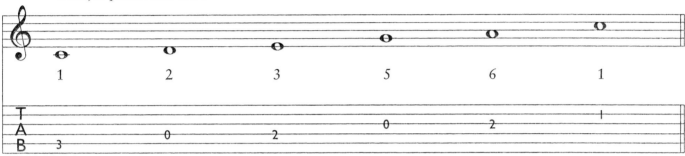

Minor Pentatonic, or Blues, Scales

By taking the relative minor of the major pentatonic scale, you can produce a *minor pentatonic,* or *blues,* scale. Thus the C major pentatonic above becomes an A blues scale by starting it on A.

A minor pentatonic (blues) scale

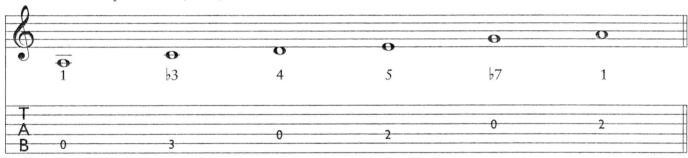

The reason that the minor pentatonic scale is good for blues lies in its flatted third—flatted in comparison to the third of the major scale. In blues—and, consequently in most rock—the third degree is often ambiguous; neither major nor minor, but somewhere in between. On guitar, this effect is easy to produce with string bending.

In addition to the ambiguous "blue" third, the pentatonic blues scale is commonly ornamented by adding the normal major third and the flatted fifth.

A blues scale with major third and flatted fifth

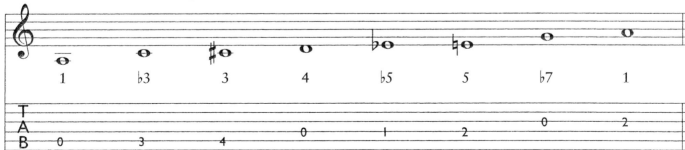

Besides being used in traditional and progressive blues, the pentatonic blues scale is commonly found in heavy metal music and all other types of rock, as well as some types of jazz.

Jazz Scales

There are many theories concerning the application of scales to jazz improvisation—some say there are as many theories as there are jazz players. The brief descriptions of how the following scales are commonly used should not therefore be taken as gospel, but rather as springboards to your further investigation of jazz theory.

Jazz Melodic Minor

As stated above, a *jazz melodic minor* scale is nothing more than a traditional melodic minor scale with the same formula descending as ascending (see "Minor Scales" above). The jazz melodic minor scale may be used to generate the *Lydian flat-seven* scale (see below).

Lydian Flat-Seven Scales

The *Lydian flat-seven* scale is generally used for soloing over dominant seventh chords other than the V chord of the progression (for which the Mixolydian scale usually suffices). The formula of the scale reveals it to be a cross between a Mixolydian and a Lydian scale, containing a flatted seventh and a sharped fourth (as compared to a major scale). This scale may also be thought of as the Lydian mode of the jazz melodic minor.

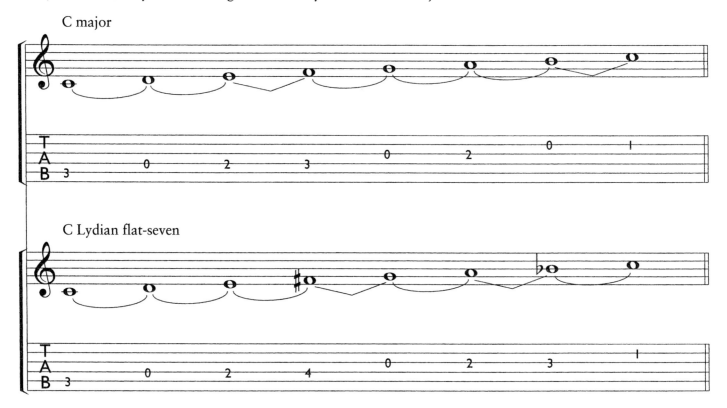

Diminished Scales

Like the chromatic scale, the *diminished* scale is a symmetrical scale, in that more than one note in the scale may be considered the root. Since its formula is a repeating alternation of whole-step/half-step, starting on every other degree will yield three other scales with identical formulas. Because of this, the C diminished scale shown below could also be considered an E-flat diminished scale, a G-flat diminished scale, or an A diminished scale.

C diminished scale

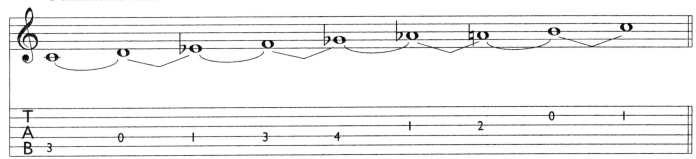

In addition to being used to solo over diminished seventh chords, the diminished scale is often used over dominant seventh chords to add tensions (flat-nine, sharp-nine, sharp-eleven, and thirteen). When used in this way, the root of the diminished scale should be one half-step above the root of the seventh chord.

Whole-Tone Scales

Another symmetrical scale is the *whole-tone* scale. Where the formula of the chromatic scale comprises all half steps and that of the diminished scale consists of alternating whole and half steps, all intervals in the whole-tone scale are whole steps.

C whole-tone scale

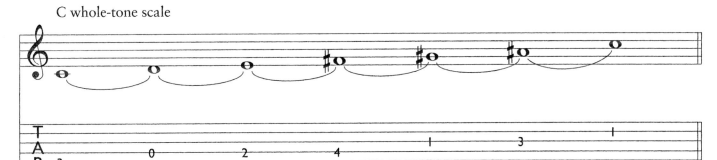

This scale goes well with augmented seventh chords because it contains all the tones of the chord plus the ninth and the sharped eleventh.

Altered Scales

Combining the first half of the diminished scale with the second half of the whole-tone scale (one half-step above) yields the *altered* scale, used against dominant seventh chords altered with the tensions flat-five, sharp-five, flat-nine, sharp-nine, and/or sharp eleven.

C altered scale

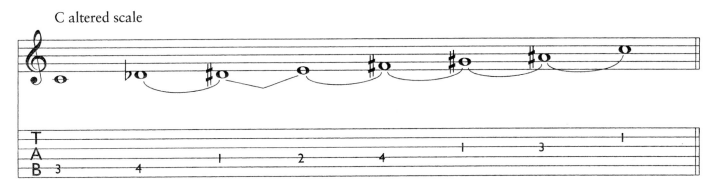

Notice that the formula of the diminished-scale portion of the C altered scale above shows it to be based on a D-flat diminished scale, even though it starts on C, a half step below. Notice also that while the diminished scale has eight steps per octave and the whole-tone scale only six, the altered scale has seven steps per octave just like the standard major, minor, and modal scales.

How to Practice Scales

Practicing scales is a perfect form of musical exercise: It combines dexterity and two-hand coordination exercise with development of velocity, strength, and endurance. In addition, there is valuable ear training and rhythmic discipline to be gained. All of these benefits come to you more or less automatically when you practice regularly and correctly. The good news is that there is no one correct way to practice and that the best method for you is one that you develop for yourself. The key is to get organized and stick to your organization. As you know by now, when it comes to your playing, you will always be your own most severe critic. Use these critical faculties to help you stay on the right track.

Here are some suggestions—some specific, some general that will help you develop your personal regimen. Pay careful attention to all them—in fact, be sure to apply each one of them sooner or later.

- If you practice an hour a day, ten to fifteen minutes should be spent on scales. Adjust this time period up or down proportionately to the total time you practice each day.

- Start out each session with something easy and familiar to you— say, a one-octave major-scale pattern moved chromatically (fret by fret) up and down the fingerboard.

- Sing every scale as you play it. This is especially beneficial when learning new fingering patterns for familiar-sounding scales as it aids your sense of ear-hand coordination. This is the skill that enables accomplished improvisers to spontaneously play any melodic ideas that they can imagine.

- Alternate playing mechanically and musically. Try variations of phrasing and articulation ranging from robotic staccato to expressive, flowing legato.

- Use a metronome or drum machine. Good sense of tempo and rhythm is essential to all music. A metronome will help you keep track of your progress as you increase speed. Remember, never practice anything faster than you can play it well.

- Try using the metronome (or drum machine) to give you the tempo, then turn it off and play a scale or scale exercise. As you finish, turn the metronome back on and see if you ended at the same tempo as you started. (This is a killer at extremely slow tempo—try it!)

- Play cross-rhythms against a drum machine. For example, play a triplet pattern while the drum machine plays a straight eighth-note pattern so that you are playing three against two. Or play straight eighth notes to the drum machine's shuffle pattern so that you are playing two against three.

- Play familiar patterns backwards or from different starting points. We tend to think of scales as going up then down. To add variety, start at the top and go down then up. If you want to find out how well you really know a particular fingering pattern, start it somewhere in the middle.

- Use scales to learn new right-hand techniques. If you play primarily with a pick, explore the fingerstyle patterns given below, or vice versa. Choose familiar scale patterns, for which the left-hand part is totally automatic.

Practice Patterns for All Scales

The practice patterns given below fall into two general categories: patterns for ordering tones within a scale and patterns for ordering the scales themselves. Using the different suggestions, or any patterns that you come up with, in various combinations can help to keep scale practice interesting and challenging.

Since it is in the nature of these patterns to be repetitive, some of them are written out in somewhat abbreviated forms. In all cases, though, you will find enough to give you the idea.

Patterns for Ordering Scale Tones

The following ideas for practice patterns have been developed with several goals in mind: Some of them are designed to be easy to learn and remember, making them excellent choices for quick warm-ups. Others will take some time to understand and master, making them better at providing more in-depth exploration of the fingerboard. After looking these patterns over, you will no doubt see how easy it is to come up with your own variations or original ideas. The trick is to try to inject some musicality into what is essentially a mathematical sequence.

All of the following examples are based on this simple C major scale pattern.

Be sure to apply them to any other major and minor scale patterns you know or are trying to learn. Most of them may be adapted to chromatic, diminished, whole-tone, and altered scales as well.

Eighth-Note Patterns

These patterns are all written out in straight eighth notes. You may play them as written, or impose a different rhythm or accent pattern on them. For example, you might choose to play the patterns in "swing eighth notes":

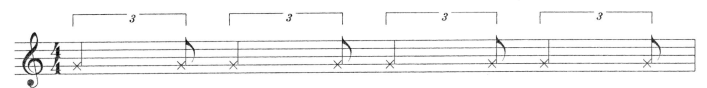

Or you could dictate a rhythmic pattern such as the following, which is reminiscent of a Scottish hornpipe.

As far as your right hand goes, use any or all of the pick and fingerstyle patterns suggested below—or come up with your own patterns based on movements that you are trying to master.

Pick-Style Alternation Patterns

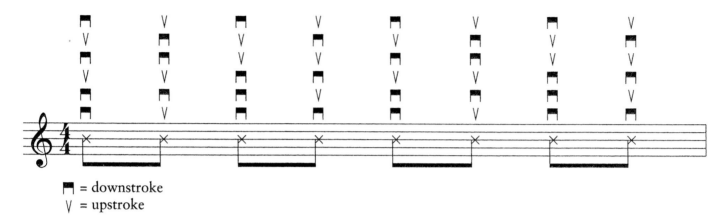

■ = downstroke
V = upstroke

Fingerstyle Alternation Patterns

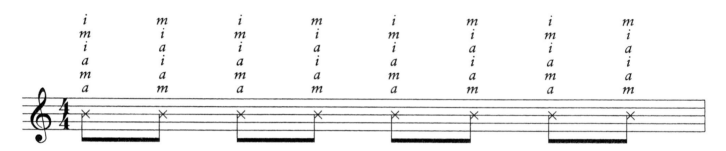

i = index finger
m = middle finger
a = ring finger

Here are a few ideas derived from various interval skips.

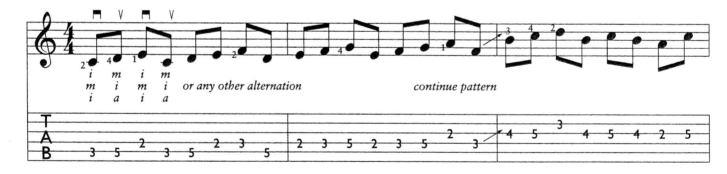

The following patterns employ repeated motifs—try using hammerons and pulloffs (indicated by slurs in the examples) wherever possible to build strength.

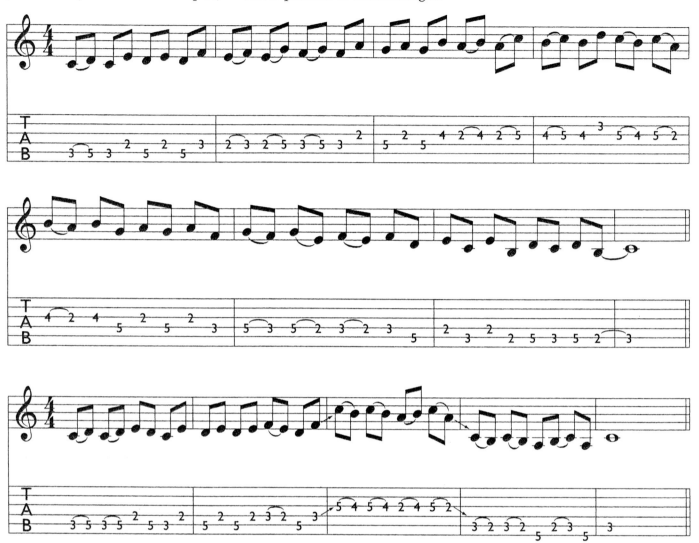

Outlining the chords contained within a scale is good ear-training practice. Watch out for the way that these patterns reverse at the top.

triads

sevenths

Triplet Patterns

Patterns based on triplet rhythms force you to deal with a whole other set of accent figures. You can use the same right-hand alternation patterns given above for the eighth-note patterns, and, in addition, you may want to apply some of these.

Pick-Style Alternation Patterns

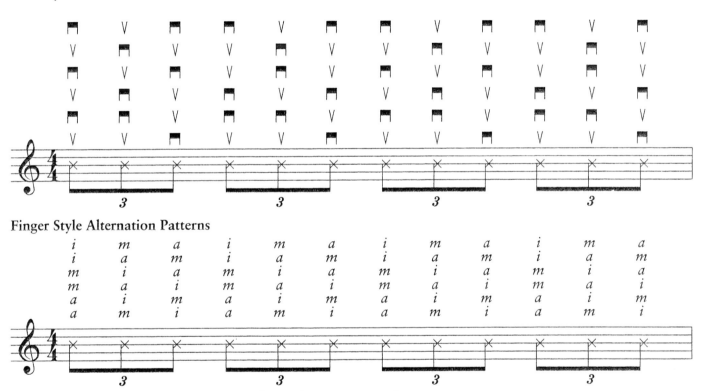

Finger Style Alternation Patterns

You can impose rhythmic variations on the triplet patterns in the same way as was outlined above for the eighth-note patterns. Here are a couple of variations you might try.

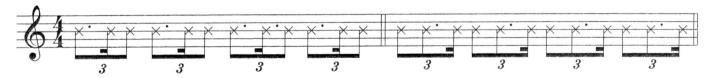

A good way to get into triplet patterns is simply to play a scale in triplets. Remember to try all of the different alternation patterns. (In the following example, notice how the in-position C major scale has been expanded to its upper and lower limits.)

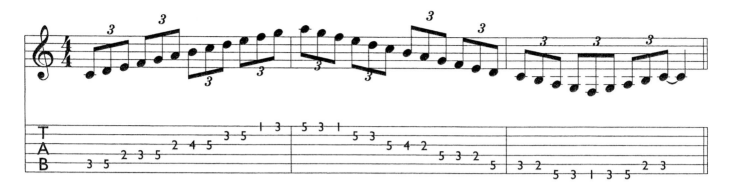

The following employ various techniques of repetition and interval skips to produce useful practice patterns.

A Melodic Alternative

Probably the most musical way to generate practice patterns is to simply play a simple diatonic melody or melodic fragment starting on each note of the scale. You could also play the tune using different scale forms. In fact, playing the same melody out of several different scale patterns is a good way to get familiar with the melody as well as with the scale pattern. Here is an example using a Charlie Parker riff which stays within a major scale.

Patterns for Ordering Scales

The two categories of patterns for ordering scales are those that provide an order for a single scale fingering and those that provide an order for a series of scales. The simplest configuration of the former category is to move a scale form up and down by half steps; that is, one fret at a time. Starting in fifth or seventh position can add some variety and make a new fingering easier to learn.

Other good patterns for this type of practice would consist of interval skips such as going up by whole steps or going up a whole step and down a half step.

To practice different scale forms, the easiest order to use is that of the circle of fifths. Try this with any one quality of scale—major, diminished, pentatonic, etc. Pick the appropriate form and starting point for each scale to give you a pattern that stays close to one position or one that jumps around a lot.

Classical guitarists have long practiced major scales and their relative melodic minor scales around the circle of fifths in this pattern.

C	A minor
G	E minor
D	B minor
A	F-sharp minor
E	C-sharp minor
B	G-sharp minor
F-sharp	D-sharp minor
D-flat	B-flat minor
A-flat	F minor
E-flat	C minor
B-flat	G minor
F	D minor

This is an excellent way to make sure that you hit every key.

The Scales

In-Position Major Scales

These scales are remarkably versatile tools. They give you seven starting points for basic major scales within one position on the neck. They are all moveable forms (containing no open strings), and each one covers a little over two octaves. If you really have a command of these forms, you will find that you can play any major (or modal) scale within one fret of any position you may be in. Note that although each of these stays within one four-fret position, some of them contain stretches up with the fourth finger or down with the first finger. These stretches are indicated by the letter *s*.

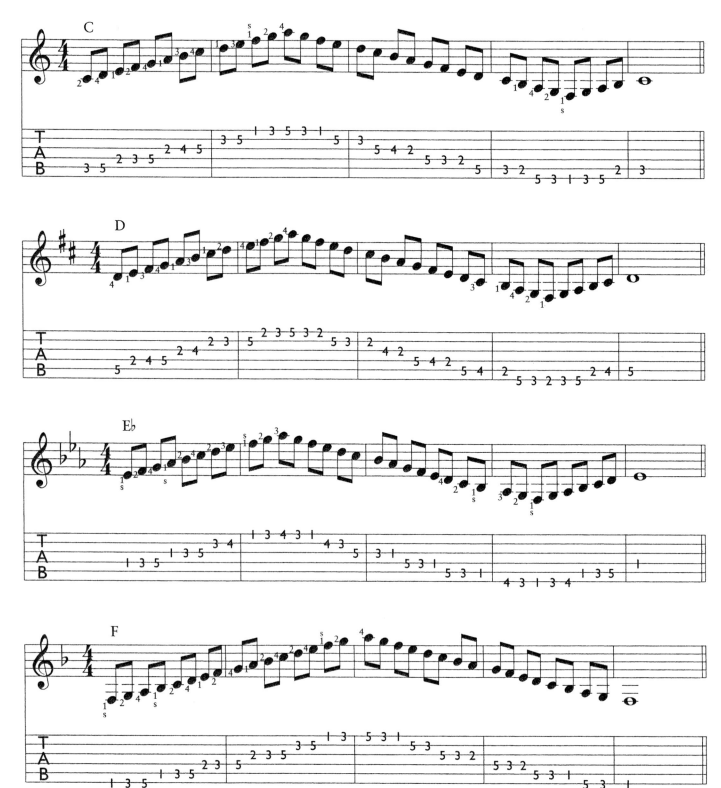

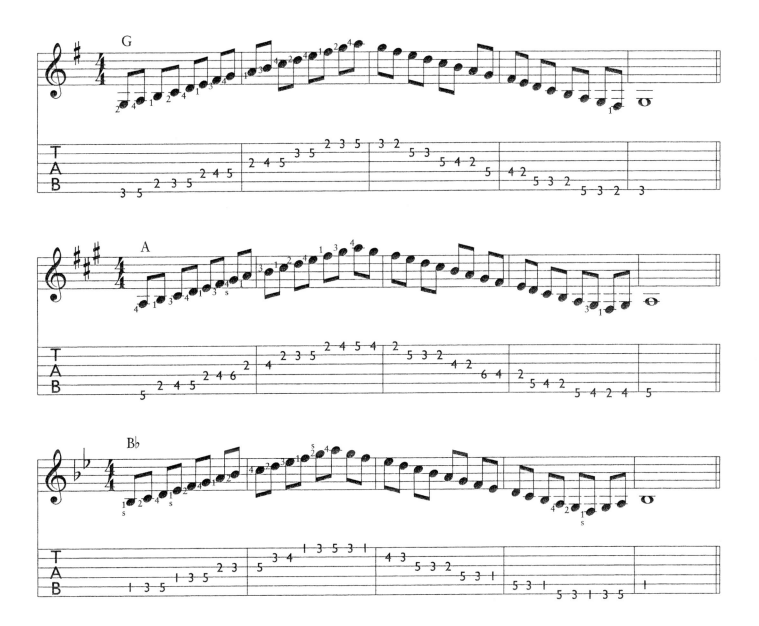

Here's an idea for practicing these scales that will really get them under your fingers: Play each scale form starting from the same root. For example, if you were to start from G-flat, the C scale form would be moved to eighth position, the D scale form to sixth position, the E-flat to fifth position, and so on. This would give you the G-flat scale in all seven positions.

In-Position Minor Scales

Any of the major-scale forms above may be transformed into a natural minor scale by simply starting on the sixth degree; thus C major becomes A natural minor, D major becomes B minor, E-flat major becomes C minor, and so on. Since the harmonic and melodic minor scale forms require different fingerings, they are written out below.

Harmonic Minor Scales

To produce harmonic minor scales, you simply sharp the seventh degree.

A harmonic minor

B harmonic minor

C harmonic minor

D harmonic minor

E harmonic minor

F# harmonic minor

G harmonic minor

Melodic Minor Scales

Remember that there are two kinds of melodic minor scales and that the forms in this book are of the "traditional" variety. If you want to practice jazz melodic minor scales, use the same fingering descending as ascending.

A melodic minor

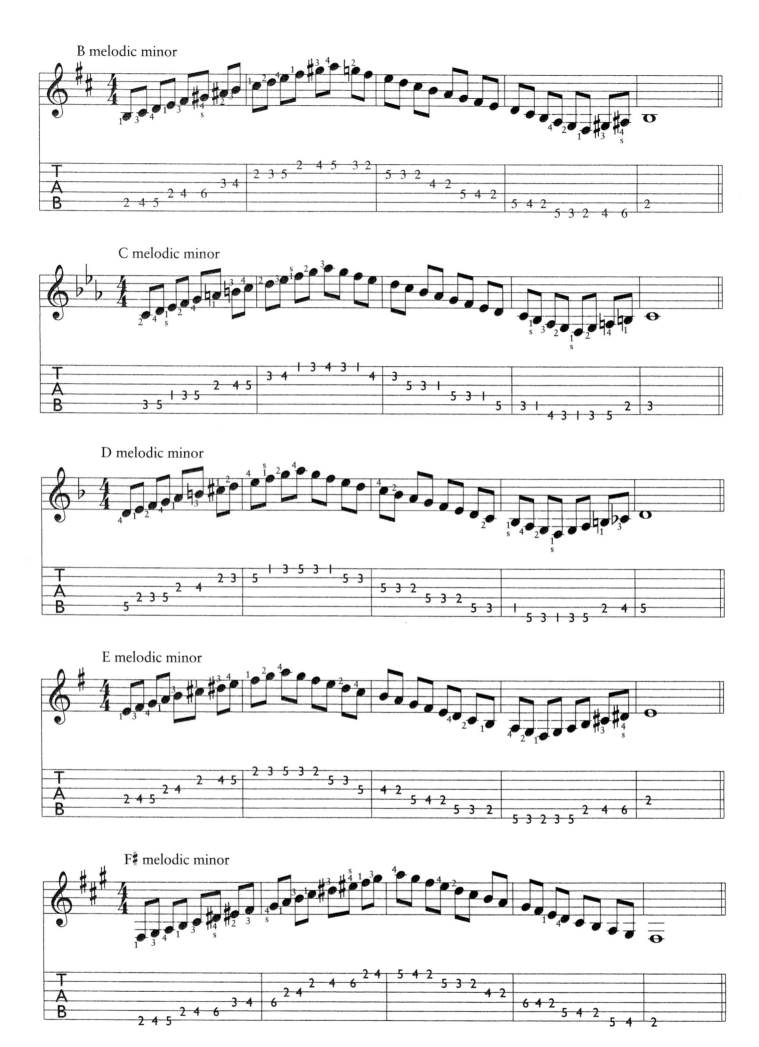

G melodic minor

Chromatic Scales

Since the chromatic scale has no real tonal center, there is no need to present forms with different starting points. The following two forms differ only in fingering.

Chromatic

Chromatic

Rock Scales

You can derive pentatonic scales from any major or minor scale by just taking the appropriate five tones and leaving out the rest (as outlined above in the "Scale Theory" section). The following are the most often used forms of these scales.

Major Pentatonic Scales

G major pentatonic
(in - position)

C major pentatonic
(in - position)

G major pentatonic
(with position shifts)

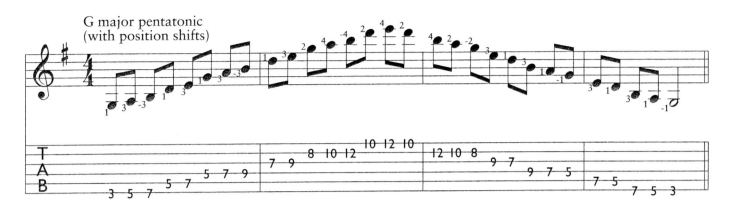

C major pentatonic
(with position shifts)

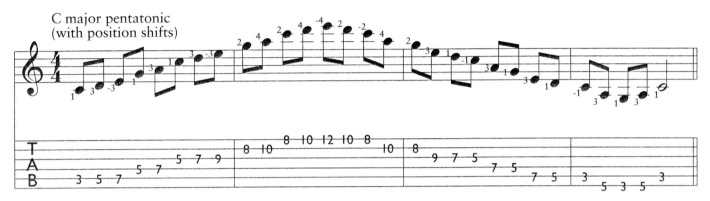

Minor Pentatonic Scales

G minor pentatonic
(in - position)

C minor pentatonic
(in - position)

E minor pentatonic
(with position shifts)

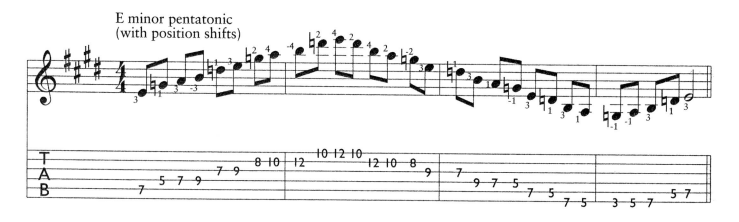

A minor pentatonic
(with position shifts)

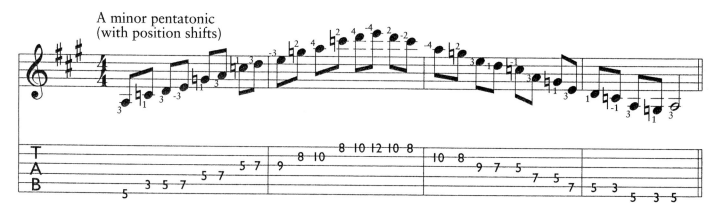

Blues Scales with Major Third and Flatted Fifth

G blues scale with major third and flatted fifth
(in - position)

C blues scale with major third and flatted fifth
(in - position)

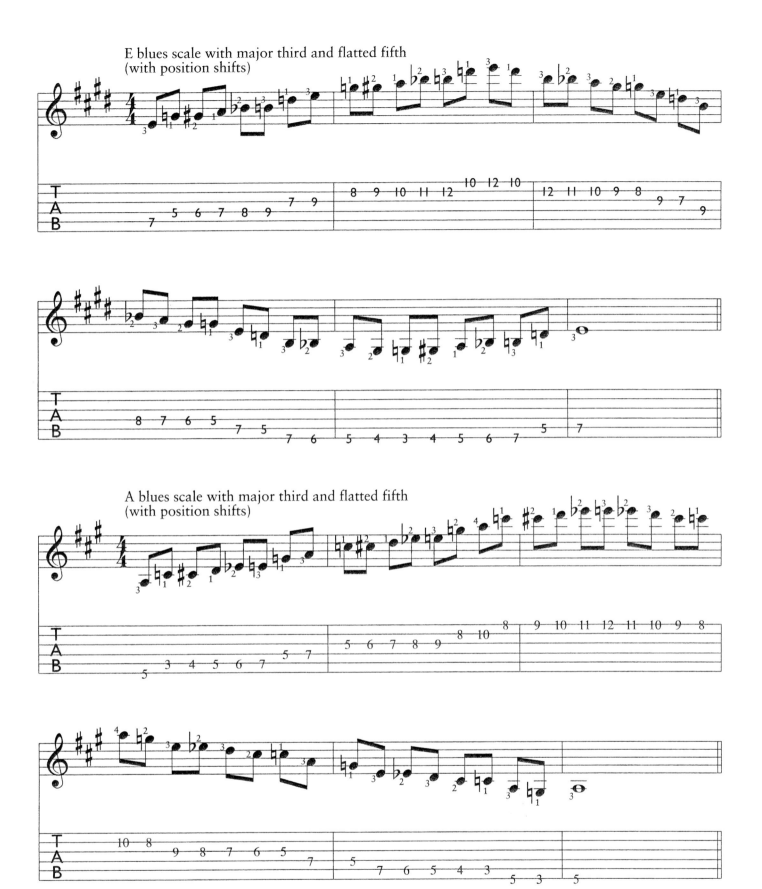

Jazz Scales

Since the jazz melodic minor scale is so similar to the traditional melodic minor, it is not necessary to detail any new forms for it. Let's take a look at the Lydian mode of the jazz melodic minor, known as the Lydian flat-seven.

Lydian Flat-Seven Scales

Compare these in-position forms to the melodic minor forms given above to understand their modal connection.

C Lydian flat-seven

G Lydian flat-seven

Diminished Scales

Here are two common in-position fingerings and one "sliding scale" fingering for the diminished scale. Remember that every other note may be considered the root, so practice these forms with different starting points to learn them thoroughly.

G, B♭, C♯, or E diminished

C, E♭, G♭, or A diminished

G, B♭, C♯, or E diminished

Whole-Tone Scales

Since the whole-tone scale has a perfectly symmetrical formula, what was said about the diminished scales above goes double here: Practice these forms considering each and every scale tone as the root.

G, A, B, C♯, D♯, or F whole-tone

C, D, E, G♭, A♭, or B♭ whole-tone

G, A, B, C♯, D♯, or F whole-tone

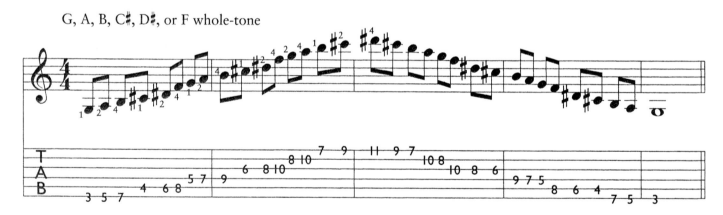

Altered Scales

Here are four good in-position patterns for altered scales.

C altered

G altered

C altered

Ideas for Extended Scales

If one of the reasons that you practice scales is to help you learn the fingerboard, then developing fingerings for extended, or *up-and-across,* scales should be one of your priorities. The idea behind this type of scale pattern is to start on the lowest note on your instrument that is part of the scale and play the scale through to the highest note on the instrument that is part of the scale. The better your understanding of the scale's formula, the easier it will be to come up with a workable fingering for an extended version of that scale.

Following are three examples of up-and-across fingerings; one each for a major, a melodic minor, and an altered scale. After mastering these, try creating your own by following the guidelines below.

C major (extended)

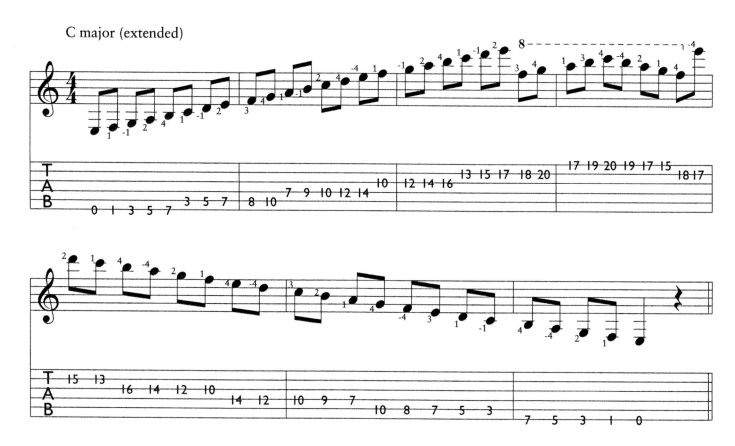

G melodic minor (extended)

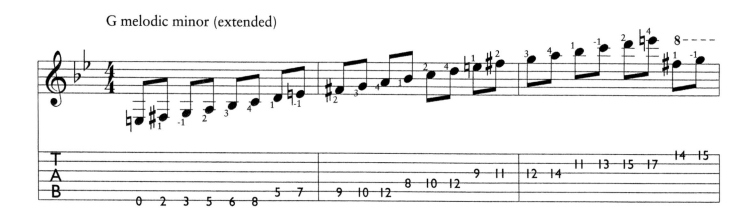

F altered (extended)

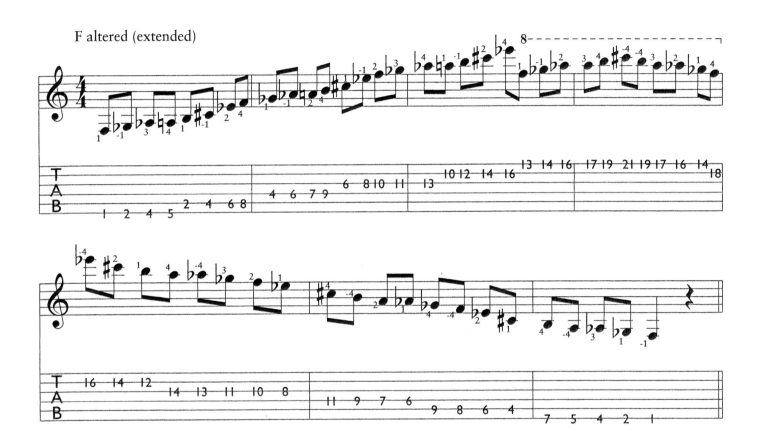

As you may have deduced from studying the above patterns, the rules for creating up-and-across fingering patterns are rather loose. The idea is to space out the notes of the scale across the entire fingerboard, avoiding a concentration in any one position. The general rules are to start on low E or F, then use a fingering pattern similar to one of the ones in the scales above. After playing four to six notes of the scale on the sixth string, move across to the fifth string and find the next note of the scale with your first finger. Then, slide up one or two frets to find the next note of the scale on the fifth string. At this point you can use any fingering pattern that will allow you to play the next three or four notes in the scale. Repeat this procedure, always sliding up every time you move across, until you reach the absolute highest note in the scale possible on the guitar.

Coming back down, reverse the process so that you are always sliding down to find the next lowest note in the scale with your fourth finger each time you move across to the next lowest string. Notice that you will always have to derive a descending pattern different from the ascending one in an extended-scale fingering pattern.

There will be many variations on these fingering patterns that you will be able to discover, and it is positively valuable to practice different up-and-across patterns for the same scale.

I hope that the scales and concepts presented in this little volume will help you to reach a better understanding of scale construction, theory, and usage. I know that you will see and feel a tremendous improvement in your playing and in your command of the fretboard if you apply these ideas, many of which are just the starting points for further study or practice. There are many excellent sources available that will allow you to learn more scales and how the different types of scales may be applied in improvisation and composition. For now, good luck—and keep practicing and playing.